Deutsche Bank

The publisher gratefully acknowledges Deutsche Bank for their support

WILDLIFE RESERVES OF INDIA

SUNJOY MONGA

INDIA BOOK HOUSE PVT LTD

CONTENTS

Introduction

India spreads over an area of almost 3.29 million sq km, encompassing a gamut of habitats that sustain a sizeable percentage of the world's faunal and floral wealth. Its avian diversity doubles that of Europe, and conservative estimates attribute about 10 per cent each of the world's mammalian, insect and fish species, and over 8 per cent of reptile forms to India. Despite this incredible natural wealth, wildlife is rarely a priority for the average tourist to India, belying the fascination that it long held for *shikaris* of the colonial era.

After independence in 1947, a spate of ill-advised developmental schemes, an uncontrolled push for agricultural land, and unmonitored hunting wrought havoc on the wilderness. The ensuing degradation of wild habitats finally prompted official action. A wilderness area in the United Provinces had already been declared a sanctuary in 1936 to deter indiscriminate hunting, and some scattered protected areas were reserved as hunting grounds for India's royalty and their privileged guests. Guided by these precedents, the administration assigned special protection to an increasing number of wilderness areas and today, the country's finest wildlife specimens are encountered within the 571 parks and sanctuaries maintained by forest departments across India.

The large number of protected areas indicates a widespread concern for conservation. However, not all bio-geographic provinces have received adequate attention, and vital habitats have been left unprotected. As many as 105 of India's protected areas are located in the Andaman and Nicobar archipelago alone, but sanctuaries occupy only a miniscule percentage of mainland India's lengthy coastline of over 7000 km. There are very few wildlife reserves in northeastern India or in the vast northern plains. Protected areas together account for barely 4 per cent of mainland India, and many of them are small; 113 sites are less than 20 sq km in extent, and some of these are too isolated from other wilderness sites to form viable habitats. With the rising demands of a burgeoning human population, only 25 wildlife reserves in India cover more than 1000 sq km each.

Conservation interests are adversely affected by the country's need for civic, agricultural and industrial development. When forests are felled, not just the trees, but entire systems of flora and fauna disappear. Similarly, when wetlands are reclaimed, the natural habitat of the mightiest of predators to the smallest of insects is wiped out. While inaccessibility can create a relatively undisturbed habitat, it also leads to shortfalls in management and supervision.

The increasing number of visitors to protected areas is cause for both celebration and concern. Forest and wildlife officials have to strike a difficult balance between ensuring the health of the reserves without drastically disturbing the inflow of tourists. As Henry David Thoreau proclaims in *Walden*, "In Wildness is the preservation of the World." Not only do national parks and sanctuaries serve as the last repositories of our natural

Peering out onto an uncertain future, the master predator takes cover in a tangle of forest undergrowth.

heritage, but they also provide employment and generate much-needed revenue. Whereas the wilderness is known to enhance our sense of well-being, human insensitivity is often counter-productive to conservation interests. Littering, overcrowding and fire are often the unfortunate side-effects of tourism.

India's protected areas are all significant in their own special way. The ones included in this work span the northern, western, central, eastern and southern zones of India and have been chosen for either their ecological importance or their tourist infrastructure. Mammals, reptiles and birds commonly seen in each reserve or vital indicators of the habitat's health have been listed under **key species**.

Areas assigned **wildlife sanctuary** status constitute habitats of ecological significance and are protected by state governments. Human activities, such as livestock grazing, collection of forest produce and tourism, within the sanctuary's precincts are monitored by the chief wildlife warden. **National parks** are given the highest level of legal protection as they provide habitats of special zoological, floral, geomorphological and ecological significance. They usually form the

The Malabar Giant Squirrel of southern India has been known to attain a length over one metre.

focal area of Project Tiger reserves. In India's 80 national parks, human activity is confined to management duties and controlled tourism, strictly enforced by law.

The **core** of a protected area receives the most stringent care. Apart from management inputs, no human activity, not even tourism,

Fresh tiger pugs on a forest trail are indicative of a healthy habitat.

may be allowed here, ensuring that at least a small part of the wilderness is left almost totally undisturbed. **Buffer** areas, on the other hand, permit controlled tourism, livestock grazing and other pastoral activities. They constitute the peripheral tracts of protected areas and often have a sanctuary component.

There are 28 **Project Tiger reserves** in India, each comprising an existing national park and adjoining tracts of land, with the primary aim of maintaining a viable tiger population. They are administered jointly by the wildlife departments of both the state and the centre. Project Tiger, initiated in 1973, is one of the most comprehensive conservation efforts ever launched. At the apex of a complex biota, the tiger can be saved, not in isolation, but by making its habitat sacrosanct. Populations of rhinoceros, elephant, swamp deer, gaur and several other species have been preserved in this way.

Photography has contributed to increasing public awareness of conservation efforts.

People form an integral part of any ecosystem. To involve them in
a region's conservation initiatives and so provide a sustainable
approach to biodiversity, UNESCO launched the Man and Biosphere
Project in 1972. A **biosphere reserve** in India is often a mix of
existing national parks and sanctuaries, with a wide transition zone
where local communities are allowed to go about their daily
activities, such as agriculture and livestock grazing. Twelve biosphere
reserves have been established in India, but only the 5,520 sq km
Nilgiri Biosphere Reserve has been registered with UNESCO.
The rest are still managed by committees with no legal protection.

   A **world heritage site** is selected by an intergovernmental
committee as a natural or cultural site of "outstanding universal value

*India is a bird-watcher's paradise, with over 1,200 avifaunal species, including the ubiquitous
Indian Peafowl (above) and the long-necked Darter (facing page).*

and exceptional interest" under threat of damage in a rapidly
developing world. India has been an active member of the world
heritage group since 1977, and among its 22 designated sites are the
wilderness areas of Manas, Kaziranga, Keoladeo Ghana, Sundarbans,
and Nanda Devi. To ensure their preservation, the government
works in close coordination with the International Union for the
Conservation of Nature and Natural Resources.

The concerted effort of visitor and bureaucrat, agriculturist and
politician, educationist and technocrat is required to preserve India's
wilderness areas and guarantee their denizens a fair chance of
survival. This book will hopefully promote wildlife tourism and
create an awareness of the rationale behind conservation efforts. Only
then can today's children learn of nature's bounties and the dangers
inherent in tampering with the wilderness. Once this lesson becomes
a *mantra*, the success of the conservation movement is ensured.

NORTHERN ZONE

From the barren heights of Ladakh, stretching along the forested Himalayan ranges, across Punjab to north-west Uttar Pradesh, the northern zone drops to India's vast and densely populated plains. It hosts an impressive array of wildlife reserves, amongst them India's first national park, Corbett, and the World Heritage Site of Bharatpur's Keoladeo Ghana National Park. A smattering of wetlands attracts some of the greatest congregations of migratory waterfowl.

DACHIGAM NATIONAL PARK

Flanked by the majestic Himalayan range, the Dachigam National Park
nestles in the Kashmir Valley, 22 km north-east of Srinagar, past the
celebrated Dal Lake. It is a stunningly picturesque park with its upper
slopes laden with flowers between May and August, and its forests turning
orange, russet, scarlet and yellow in autumn. Of tremendous conservation
significance, Dachigam's temperate and broad-leaved forests and grassy
meadows constitute nearly half the catchment area of the Dal Lake. The
Dagwan River originates in the park's higher reaches to flow through its
rocky and forested slopes before draining into the lake.

Dachigam is the world's last stronghold of the Hangul, or Kashmir
Stag. On the verge of extinction, the deer's population dipped to 180 in
the early 1970s. Strict management succeeded in saving the ungulate,
a subspecies of the European Red Deer, from extinction, but subsequent
political unrest in the region may have undermined conservation efforts.
A big stag can be a very dark brown, specially with his thick winter coat,
but turns paler in summer. There are usually five points on each antler, but
up to eight points have been reported. Fawns tend to have spotted coats.

The Dagwan River flows through Dachigam before draining into the Dal Lake.

The royal family of Kashmir first offered protection to the area as a game reserve in the early 1900s. Over the years, adjoining grassy slopes and high-altitude lakes were included in the reserve, so that today the altitudinal range of the park, demarcated into Upper and Lower Dachigam, extends from 1,700 to 4,200 m. Silver birch, blue pine and juniper mingle with pasture, scrubland and barren rock in the higher reaches, while fir, spruce and pine forest the middle altitudes, turning to broad-leaved oak, walnut and horse-chestnut with plenty of undergrowth in the lower region. Himalayan Black Bear feast on the fruiting oak, walnut and horse-chestnut between late August and early October before hibernating for the winter. The upper reaches are rendered inaccessible by winter snow and most of the wildlife descends to more hospitable areas.

This is an excellent park for trekking and camping. Sightings of Snow Leopard have been reported, but on common view are a wide range of other mammals, such as Leopard and Hill Fox, and over 150 species of birds including Himalayan Monal and Koklass Pheasant. This is also the breeding area for several species of warblers that winter in peninsular India. The most impressive draw, however, is the Kashmir Stag, his widespread antlers a frequent sight in the forest and surrounding grassy slopes.

KEY SPECIES

MAMMALS Hangul (Kashmir Stag) (*above*), Himalayan Black Bear, Brown Bear, Himalayan Tahr, Leopard, Hill Fox, Yellow-throated Marten, Leopard-cat, Serow, Goral, Musk Deer, Himalayan Marmot, Wild Boar, Jackal, Common Langur

BIRDS RAPTORS Lammergeier, Himalayan Griffon, Golden Eagle, Common Kestrel, Northern Goshawk, Tawny Owl

ALPINE/WOODLAND/SCRUB Himalayan Monal (*below*), Koklass Pheasant, Kalij Pheasant, Yellow-billed Blue Magpie, Red-billed Chough, Yellow-billed Chough, Spotted Nutcracker, Ultramarine Flycatcher, Long-tailed Minivet, Wallcreeper, Himalayan Woodpecker, White-cheeked Nuthatch, Streaked Laughingthrush, Variegated Laughingthrush, Black-and-yellow Grosbeak

WATERSIDE White-capped Water Redstart, Plumbeous Water Redstart, Little Forktail, Spotted Forktail, Brown Dipper

Additional information on page 114

HEMIS NATIONAL PARK

A kaleidoscope of visual images, the cold and windy Hemis National Park is a land of splendid ruggedness. Snow-clad peaks soar against azure skies, sunlight breaks vividly on the bare mountain slopes, narrow rivers cut sharply through shadowy chasms and stark ridges rise knife-like from the landscape. The ecology of this barren region hangs in a fine balance, easily disturbed by the poacher or the insensitive tourist.

The national park is named after a Buddhist monastery, the Hemis Gompa, situated near the park. The area of Hemis extends over 4,100 sq km in the trans-Himalayan Ladakh district of Jammu and Kashmir, encompassing the Markha and Rumbak Valleys and the twisting Zanskar River, which cuts a dramatic gorge. With an altitudinal range of 3,300 to 6,000 m, this cold desert hosts a remarkable variety of wildlife. The rarefied air and low temperatures are a constant challenge, but this almost treeless realm is a supreme example of nature's adaptability.

The key predator in the park, the endangered Snow Leopard, is an elusive but beautiful sight. Its thick coat of grey, fading to white on its underbelly, and pale markings are an excellent camouflage in the dappled landscape of snow and rock. The inaccessibility of its haunts keeps it

Between May and August, vivid flowers enliven the barren landscape of Hemis.

largely hidden from human eyes. Intrepid poachers, braving the terrain and the biting winds, have been known to seek out the leopard for its highly prized fur. Research has revealed a possible Snow Leopard population of 30-50 within the park. Other hunters are the Wolf and the Red Fox. In the 1980s, a pack of four Wild Dogs was spotted in the Markha Valley.

The Bharal, or Blue Sheep, grazes on the rich grasses of the higher levels of Hemis during summer. Its population in the park is about 4,000. There are fewer Ibex, sturdy goats with rather long horns, while two sheep, the small Ladakh Urial with heavily wrinkled horns and the Tibetan Argali, are on the endangered list, the former with a population of only about 300. But several rodents, such as mice and voles, and other small animals, such as tailless mouse-hares, can be seen on the park's barren landscape. There are about 50 high-altitude species of birds. The park offers spectacular trekking routes, but its wildlife is not easily spotted. Moreover, because of its terrain and climate, the park has a very short visiting season.

There is local antagonism towards the Snow Leopard and the Wolf, who prey on livestock, and suspicion of the herbivores that damage crops, but ongoing efforts aim to inculcate in the people here an understanding of the intrinsic value of the park and its animals.

KEY SPECIES

MAMMALS Snow Leopard (Ounce) (*above*), Wolf, Wild Dog (Dhole), Pallas's Cat, Red Fox, Bharal (Blue Sheep), Ibex, Ladakh Urial (Shapu), Tibetan Argali, Long-tailed Marmot, Himalayan Mouse-hare
BIRDS RAPTORS Golden Eagle, Himalayan Griffon, Lammergeier, Little Owl, Common Kestrel
SCRUB/OPEN AREAS Himalayan Snowcock, Tibetan Partridge, **Chukar** (*below*), Horned Lark, Snow Pigeon, Hill Pigeon, Red-billed Chough, Yellow-billed Chough, Black-billed Magpie, Common Raven, White-tailed Rubythroat, Bluethroat, Mountain Chiffchaff, Grey Wagtail, Robin Accentor, Alpine Accentor, Tibetan Snowfinch, Rock Bunting
WATERSIDE Common Merganser, Brown-headed Gull, Brown Dipper, White-throated Dipper, White-winged Redstart

Additional information on page 115

GREAT HIMALAYAN NATIONAL PARK

The Sainj and the Tirthan are two narrow rivers that charge through the Himalayan massif and merge into the larger Beas River, about 50 km south of the popular hill resort of Kullu. The catchment forests of these two rivers and their adjoining tracts constitute the Great Himalayan National Park. Wildlife surveys in the early 1970s indicated viable populations of several endangered species in this area. Interestingly, it hosted five species of pheasants, including the vividly-coloured Western Tragopan and the Cheer Pheasant, distinctive with its long, broadly barred tail and pronounced crest. Based on detailed ecological and scientific

investigations led by Dr Anthony Gaston of the Canadian Wildlife Service, the national park was established in 1984 in this pristine wilderness of mountainous Himachal Pradesh.

Spread over 754.40 sq km, the park has a wide altitudinal range with distinct ecological layers. Snow is less frequent and heavy than in the Manali area not far to the north, but rainfall

High-altitude meadows intersperse hilly forests (above) *in the park, where the Western Tragopan* (left) *can sometimes be seen.*

is proportionately higher. Bleak and cold summits lead down to lush alpine scrublands and pastures where a few nomads graze their livestock. In the high and middle ranges, coniferous forests of birch, blue pine, deodar (the 'tree of the gods'), fir and spruce merge with forests of stately oaks, while lower down are lush broad-leaved forests of walnut, elm and horse-chestnut, crowded with ferns and mosses. Fed by ice-melts and rain, a labyrinth of torrents resounds through the park, its roar accompanying the frenzied squeals of dippers, the restless birds thriving in the freezing waters.

This is a true pheasant country and Koklass, Cheer, Kalij, Himalayan Monal and Western Tragopan are all found here, along with a variety of other woodland birds and over 40 species of mammals. The Snow Leopard may occur in the high reaches, but remains elusive. More frequently sighted are Brown Bear grazing on the fresh succulent grass of spring and early summer, and Serow, a goat-antelope species of the lower elevations. The hornless Musk Deer is also a rare sight.

The best way to explore this park is to trek up the rivers to the high pastures of Rakti Sar and Tirath. The mountains provide an unforgettable camping experience, but they are also the backdrop for intense competition between the graziers on the one hand and conservation demands on the other.

KEY SPECIES

MAMMALS Leopard, **Himalayan Black Bear** (*below*), Brown Bear, Himalayan Tahr, Goral, Serow, **Musk Deer** (*above*), Bharal (Blue Sheep), Indian Flying Squirrel, Red Fox, Himalayan Palm Civet, Leopard-cat, Himalayan Weasel

BIRDS RAPTORS Himalayan Griffon, Lammergeier, Golden Eagle, Booted Eagle, Common Kestrel, Oriental Hobby, Mountain Hawk Eagle, Collared Owlet, Tawny Owl

ALPINE/WOODLAND/SCRUB Western Tragopan, Cheer Pheasant, Koklass Pheasant, Himalayan Monal, Kalij Pheasant, Himalayan Snowcock, Hill Partridge, Yellow-billed Chough, Grandala, Spotted Nutcracker, Yellow-billed Blue Magpie, Grey Treepie, Large Hawk Cuckoo, Scaly-bellied Woodpecker, Great Barbet, Speckled Wood Pigeon, Striated Laughingthrush, Chestnut-bellied Rock Thrush, White-collared Blackbird, Plain Crossbill, Black-and-yellow Grosbeak

WATERSIDE Spotted Forktail, Brown Dipper, White-capped Water Redstart

Additional information on page 116

VALLEY OF FLOWERS NATIONAL PARK

Treks to the enchanting Valley of Flowers National Park in Uttaranchal start at Govindghat, a tiny town lying on the winding road from Rishikesh to Badrinath. The first 13 km to Ghangaria are amid stunning landscapes, then the trail narrows to steeply traverse meadow and forest to the park.

The discovery of this valley was almost accidental. Although mentioned in Hindu mythology as Nandan Kanan (the valley where gods play), its location was familiar only to local pastoralists to whom it was the Bhyundhar Valley. In 1931, Frank S Smythe, a British mountaineer, and his four companions lost their way in bad weather whilst returning from an expedition to Mt Kamet. When the mists cleared, they found themselves in a profusion of flowers. Fascinated, Smythe revisited the valley in 1937 and, in the following year, introduced it to the modern world in his book, *The Valley of Flowers*. To him it was "a valley of peace and perfect beauty where the human spirit may find repose."

In 1982, an area of 87.50 sq km in the Chamoli district was declared the Valley of Flowers National Park. Satellite images show that over 63 sq km of this area is under perpetual snow. Forests constitute 5.29 sq km and alpine meadows, where the wealth of species bloom, cover 18.63 sq km.

During July and August, balsams are amongst the many flowers seen in profusion.

The valley, 3,360–3,900 m high, offers a panoramic view of the peaks around it, with Gauri Parbat (6,590 m) and Rataban (6,126 m) towering in the east, Kunt Khal (4,430 m) in the west, Saptsring (5,038 m) in the south and Nilgiri Parbat (6,479 m) in the north. An approximately 8 km long glacial corridor, the valley measures almost 2 km at its widest part.

The park hosts over 500 species of plants, many of great medicinal importance. Over the years, several species have become depleted and a few are actually endangered. Asters, balsams, calendulas, dandelions, edelweisses, gentians, irises, senecios and windflowers are just some of the flowers that appear as the snow melts. In the monsoon months, from mid-July to late August, they display a staggering burst. A medley of butterflies and other insects come alive with the flowering, and many Himalayan birds breed during this period. The herbivorous Himalayan Black Bear comes out to graze in this time of plenty. Sightings of Brown Bear and Serow have been reported.

Excessive human intrusion over a period of time has seriously endangered the valley's floral and faunal denizens, including the Musk Deer. To safeguard this unique natural heritage, trekking, camping and various other activities have been banned since the mid-1980s and only daytime access is allowed to this incredible park.

KEY SPECIES

MAMMALS Leopard, Himalayan Tahr, Musk Deer, Red Fox, Himalayan Weasel, Yellow-throated Marten, Himalayan Black Bear, Brown Bear, Himalayan Mouse-hare, Bharal (Blue Sheep), Indian Flying Squirrel
BIRDS RAPTORS Lammergeier, Himalayan Griffon, Common Kestrel, Golden Eagle, Black Eagle
ALPINE/WOODLAND/SCRUB Himalayan Monal, Koklass Pheasant, Kalij Pheasant, Himalayan Snowcock, Snow Partridge, Hill Partridge, Chukar, Red-billed Chough, Yellow-billed Chough, Common Raven, Grandala, Snow Pigeon, Spotted Laughingthrush, Variegated Laughingthrush, Plain-backed Thrush, Upland Pipit, Rosy Pipit, Rock Bunting, White-capped Bunting
WATERSIDE Brown Dipper, White-throated Dipper, Spotted Forktail, Little Forktail
FLORA TREES pines, maples, firs, spruces, rhododendrons, silver birch, common yew
HERBS/SHRUBS asters, balsams, dandelions, edelweisses, gentians, geraniums, irises, lilies, poppies (**Blue Poppy** above), potentillas, primulas, saussurea, senecios

Additional information on page 116

Rajaji National Park

Less than a 20-minute drive east of the holy town of Haridwar, where the river Ganga emerges from the mountains, lies Rajaji National Park. Situated in Uttaranchal state, the park's main entrance at Ramgarh is just 15 km from Dehradun. Rajaji's forests were once contiguous with those of the Corbett Tiger Reserve, 170 km to the south-east along the Shivalik foothills, but now with spreading human settlements only isolated pockets of forest remain in the hills and the adjoining *terai* plains.

In 1984, three neighbouring sanctuaries, Rajaji, Motichur and Chilla, were merged to form the 820 sq km Rajaji National Park. The park's name is a tribute to the first Indian governor-general, the renowned freedom fighter, C Rajagopalachari. The park covers a gamut of habitats, from lush semi-evergreen forest to tall stands of deciduous sal, and from mixed broad-leaved and riverine vegetation to the characteristic *terai* grasslands. Herds of deer are often sighted on the grasslands, while sizeable numbers of Goral, a goat-antelope, keep to the low precipitous hills. The park is approximately the north-west limit of the Asian Elephant's distribution and, according to the 1999 census, hosts 445 wild elephants despite the disruption in their traditional migratory routes.

Small herds of Chital, or Spotted Deer, are frequently encountered in the Rajaji National Park.

Jeep rides are possible and walking is permitted along select routes in the park. The Wild Dog, distinctive in its deep red coat, has been sighted. A variety of other smaller carnivores flourish at Rajaji, and although 32 tigers and 177 leopards were reported in 1999, much of this park's wildlife is not very easily seen. Sightings of the nocturnal Sloth Bear are rare. Over 300 species of birds have been recorded here. Red Junglefowl can be usually spotted on many trails and the variety of woodpeckers and hornbills demonstrates the health of the forest. With regard to its avifauna, Rajaji forms an interesting zone of transition between the temperate western Himalaya and the central and eastern Himalaya. In addition, the park marks the transition zone for avifaunal species from the forested foothills to the open grasslands.

As this is an important migratory route for wildlife, special corridors were created under the busy Rishikesh-Chilla road that cuts through the park, to ensure safe passage. However, there are several instances of animals being run over by automobiles, and the railway has also had debilitating repercussions. On the night of May 28, 2001, the Mussoorie Express ran over a cow elephant in the park's Motichur area. Urgent steps are required to curb unwelcome human intrusion and the further fragmentation of animal habitats.

KEY SPECIES

MAMMALS Asian Elephant, Tiger, Goral, Leopard, Jungle Cat, Leopard-cat, Common Palm Civet, Sloth Bear, **Jackal** (*above*), Small Indian Mongoose, Common Mongoose, Barking Deer, Sambar, Spotted Deer (Chital), **Wild Boar** (*below*)

BIRDS RAPTORS Osprey, Pallas's Fish Eagle, Lesser Fish Eagle, Eurasian Marsh Harrier, Brown Fish Owl

WOODLAND/SCRUB Red Junglefowl, Indian Peafowl, Black Francolin, Oriental Pied Hornbill, Great Slaty Woodpecker, Greater Yellownape, Maroon Oriole, Large Cuckooshrike, Jungle Myna, Blue-bearded Bee-eater, Lesser Racket-tailed Drongo, Spangled Drongo, Asian Paradise-flycatcher, Crimson Sunbird

WATERSIDE Greylag Goose, Ruddy Shelduck, Comb Duck, Spotbill Duck, Stork-billed Kingfisher

Additional information on page 117

CORBETT TIGER RESERVE

The Corbett Tiger Reserve lies in the Nainital and Pauri Garhwal districts of Uttaranchal, 19 km from Ramnagar, on the road to Ranikhet. At the meeting-point of the temperate western Himalaya and the proportionately more luxuriant and tropical central Himalaya, and drained by many rivers, the park has a staggering number of species. The region once teemed with big game hunters until naturalist-*shikaris* convinced Sir Malcolm Hailey, the governor of the United Provinces, to assign a small area for special protection. India's first national park, Hailey, was established in 1936.

Post-independence, the park was renamed the Ramganga National Park after the scenic river that flows through, and later, in 1957, its name was changed to Corbett, in honour of the celebrated hunter-naturalist and writer, Jim Corbett. His winter home in Kaladhungi, just 40 km from Ramnagar, has been converted into an interesting museum. The park became part of a tiger reserve when Project Tiger was officially launched here on April 1, 1973 by the then union minister, Dr Karan Singh.

Corbett displays terrain typical of the biologically active Shivaliks (Himalayan foothills). This comprises the *terai*, or marshy alluvial plains, and the *bhabar*, densely forested fertile land rising from the *terai* to a height of 600 m. The reserve has an elevation range of 400–1,200 m. The hills, river valleys, open plateaus and ravines exhibit distinctive vegetation,

Tigers are usually easier to sight on elephant-backs in the lush forests of Corbett.

making it the "land of trumpet, roar and song." Elephants, tigers, leopards, deer, crocodiles, over 500 bird species and an assortment of floral and insect wealth make this a naturalist's Shangri La. The 30 km drive between Dhangarhi, the main entrance to the park, and Dhikala, the tourist complex at its heart, is a wildlife safari in itself. There are several other exciting routes for viewing wildlife, while rest-houses provide the experience of staying overnight in the untamed forest.

Walking is banned in most areas and wildlife can be viewed as unobtrusively as possible from elephant-backs or open jeeps. Gharials, long-snouted crocodiles, bask log-like on river-banks and bands of gleaming otters play along the edge of the flowing waters. Fresh tiger pugmarks along a forest trail provide the thrill of tracking as they indicate that the predator walked by only a short while ago. In 1997, the tiger population was reported to be 138. The wild elephant population is over 150. The Asian Elephant can be easily distinguished from its African cousin by its smaller, more convex silhouette and its smaller ears. It is believed to have a longer life span.

The thunderous trumpet of the elephant, the roar of the tiger, the flutter of wood pigeons and the shrill whistle of the soaring Crested Serpent Eagle are all familiar sounds in this most hallowed of Indian wildlife reserves.

KEY SPECIES

MAMMALS Asian Elephant (*above*), Tiger, Leopard, Leopard-cat, Fishing Cat, Jungle Cat, Wild Dog (Dhole), Gaur (Indian Bison), Sloth Bear, Himalayan Palm Civet, Smooth Indian Otter, Hog-deer, Goral, Indian Pangolin, Sambar, Spotted Deer (Chital), Barking Deer

REPTILES Mugger (Marsh Crocodile), Gharial, Indian Python

BIRDS RAPTORS Osprey, Pallas's Fish Eagle, Lesser Fish Eagle, Black Eagle, Mountain Hawk Eagle, Crested Serpent Eagle, Rufous-bellied Eagle, Crested Goshawk, Hen Harrier, Lesser Spotted Eagle, Brown Fish Owl, Brown Hawk Owl, Spot-bellied Eagle Owl

WOODLAND/SCRUB Red Junglefowl, Kalij Pheasant, Black Francolin, Great Hornbill, Oriental Pied Hornbill, Greater Yellownape, Great Slaty Woodpecker, Blue-throated Barbet, Blue-bearded Bee-eater, Chestnut-headed Bee-eater, Dollarbird, Lesser Racket-tailed Drongo, Greater Racket-tailed Drongo, Spangled Drongo, Maroon Oriole, Orange-bellied Leafbird, White-crested Laughingthrush

WATERSIDE Black-necked Stork, Black Stork, Darter, Great Cormorant, Common Merganser, Crested Kingfisher

Additional information on page 118

DUDHWA TIGER RESERVE

A timeless reminder of the rich biodiversity of the *terai's* alluvial plains, Dudhwa Tiger Reserve lies in the Lakhimpur-Kheri district of Uttar Pradesh. This area was once menaced by poachers and over-hunting and was under pressure for agricultural land and timber. It took the untiring efforts of environmentalist Billy Arjan Singh to rescue it from almost certain ruin. Declared a sanctuary in 1965 and upgraded to a national park in 1977, Dudhwa became part of a Project Tiger reserve in the late 1980s.

Dudhwa is a mix of moist grasslands and sal-dominated forests, almost contiguous with Nepal's Royal Bardia and Sukla Phanta Reserves. For part of its length the river Mohana roughly demarcates the border with Nepal. The grasslands are Dudhwa's main charm, the grass in some areas tall enough to hide an elephant. The rare Swamp Deer (Barasingha), native only to India, numbers about 1,800 here. Habitat fragmentation led to a drastic drop in its population but improved administration has helped. The Swamp Deer keep mostly to the grassy wetlands of Sathiana and Kakmha, where they feed until late in the morning and again in the evening.

The One-horned Rhinoceros is a gentle giant once widespread in the *terai* plains of Uttar Pradesh and throughout the Gangetic plains. It was hunted out of existence from the *terai* by the late 19th century.

Prime grasslands and riverine forests in Dudhwa are among the few surviving terai *wildernesses.*

Later, the Assam and West Bengal populations of this animal were seriously threatened by disease and poachers. In a bold initiative in 1985, two males and five females were transferred to Dudhwa where, by 2001, they had multiplied to 16. During the mid-1960s and early 1970s, a small herd of wild elephants was sighted here. The elusive and little-known Hispid Hare, last seen in 1951 and presumed locally extinct for years, was rediscovered in 1984. Elephants are rarely sighted today. Muggers (Marsh Crocodiles) and otters can usually be seen on the sandy banks of the rivers Mohana and Suheli, but the dense grass cover and thick woods make tiger sighting difficult. However, this is the park where Billy Arjan Singh successfully weaned the tiger cub, Tara, from being virtually domesticated to a natural life in the wilds.

Dudhwa, a blend of swamp, *jheel* (lake), grassland, riverine and forested habitats is home to nearly 400 species of birds, including the Bengal Florican, perhaps the rarest bustard in the world today. Several migratory duck, geese and various resident waterbirds are found in the wetlands while eagles, harriers and hawks circle overhead. A mélange of owls take over between dusk and dawn when several mammals are also on the move. These untamed, amazingly resilient wilds of India have survived despite intensifying human demands.

KEY SPECIES

MAMMALS One-horned Rhinoceros (*above*), Tiger, Swamp Deer (Barasingha), Hog-deer, Leopard, Leopard-cat, Fishing Cat, Jungle Cat, Common Palm Civet, Smooth Indian Otter, Sloth Bear, Sambar, Barking Deer, Spotted Deer (Chital)
REPTILES Mugger (Marsh Crocodile)
BIRDS BUSTARDS Bengal Florican
RAPTORS Pallas's Fish Eagle, Lesser Fish Eagle, Crested Serpent Eagle, Crested Goshawk, Eurasian Marsh Harrier, Hen Harrier, Brown Fish Owl
WOODLAND/SCRUB Black Francolin, Swamp Francolin, Red Junglefowl, Indian Peafowl, Oriental Pied Hornbill, Blue-bearded Bee-eater, Great Slaty Woodpecker, Greater Flameback, Streak-throated Woodpecker, Lineated Barbet, Drongo Cuckoo, Green-billed Malkoha, Striated Babbler, Yellow-bellied Prinia, Straited Grassbird, Bristled Grassbird
WATERSIDE Black-necked Stork, Black Stork, Lesser Adjutant, White Stork, Sarus Crane, Brown Crake, River Lapwing, River Tern, Cinnamon Bittern, Black Bittern, Stork-billed Kingfisher

Additional information on page 118

SARISKA TIGER RESERVE

The Sariska Tiger Reserve is steeped in history. The Mughal emperor,
Aurangzeb, is said to have imprisoned his elder brother, Dara Shikoh, in
the striking hilltop fort of Kankwadi. The ruins of a myriad Hindu and
Jain temples built between the 8th and the 12th centuries are a testimony
to the great architecture of the past. Pandupole, in the park's south-east, is
associated with the Pandavas of the Hindu epic, the *Mahabharata*. The
popular temple of the god Hanuman is a favoured spot with monkeys.

The palace built by the late Maharaja Jai Singh of Alwar between 1892
and 1902 is now largely converted into a luxury hotel. A keen *shikari*,
the maharaja ensured the protection of his private hunting reserve with
watch-towers to monitor the wildlife and waterholes to improve the
habitat. A wildlife sanctuary was declared here in 1955 and a 273.80 sq
km area was upgraded to a national park in 1992. The north-west limit of
the tiger's distribution, Sariska was included in Project Tiger in 1978-79.

Sariska, which lies in the Aravali Range of arid north-east Rajasthan,
has steep hills, low slopes and dry but dense forest covering its rugged
landscape. In the dry months of summer and winter the forest looks

In Sariska's dry and rugged terrain, waterholes are a scene of considerable animal activity.

brown and parched but is splashed with the vivid orange-red blooms of the flame of the forest tree in March-April. Troops of langurs relish their fleshy petals and birds feast on the nourishing nectar.

The forest intermingles with stretches of grassland where herbivores such as the Sambar (the largest Indian deer), the Spotted Deer or Chital, the Wild Boar and the Common Langur can be seen, usually with bands of peafowl. Nilgai (Blue Bull) and Chowsingha (Four-horned Antelope) are also common grazers, distinct from true antelopes in the structure of their horns, which are keeled in front and unringed. They are native only to India. Mistakenly classified with the cow family, the Blue Bull has largely escaped persecution. Rather like a horse in appearance, the male is much darker than the female.

The numerous waterholes get many animal visitors, especially in summer. Observation hides at Kalighati and Slopka, waterholes in the heart of the park, can be highly rewarding as there is movement all day long, the slightest sign of a predatory tiger or leopard setting off a flurry of activity. The tiger here is more crepuscular and nocturnal than in Ranthambore, 200 km to the south.

While Sariska and its wildlife have survived waves of ancient invasions, increasing human population and demands are now their greatest challenge.

Additional information on page 119

KEOLADEO GHANA NATIONAL PARK
(BHARATPUR BIRD SANCTUARY)

The Keoladeo Ghana National Park in Rajasthan is only a small area of
28.73 sq km, but its wealth of bird species has brought it prominence as
a World Heritage Site, one of only five natural history sites in India to
receive this honour. The park, better known as the Bharatpur Bird
Sanctuary, is renowned the world over for its avifauna, although a great
assortment of mammals can be sighted here as well.

Strict protection and excellent management have made Keoladeo
a haven for birds. Like several protected areas in India today, it was once
the hunting preserve of the local royal family and is probably the only
instance of a suitable habitat being 'created' by a maharaja. In the late
19th century, the arid scrublands were dramatically altered. What used to
be a seasonal, rain-filled depression became a wetland ecosystem, the
water supply augmented by diverting a nearby irrigation canal and by
conserving the existing water sources. Of course, the maharaja's intention
was to create the finest waterfowl hunting preserve in north India.
A plaque near the Keoladeo Temple within the park records the daily tally
over the years. The highest figure is of 4,273 birds in November 1938,
bagged by the then viceroy, Lord Linlithgow's party.

Bharatpur's famed heronries bustle with herons, storks and cormorants between July and October.

The renowned ornithologist
Salim Ali's efforts created an
awareness of the importance of this
area. In 1956, it was declared a
sanctuary, although 'VIP shoots'
continued until 1964 and Maharaja
Brijendra Singh retained hunting
rights until 1972. Upgraded to a
national park, this region has over
350 species of birds and about 125
breed in the park. During the
breeding season between mid-July
and early October, the crowded
nesting colonies of cormorants,
herons, egrets and storks are a scene
of endless activity as adult birds fly
all day long in an effort to satisfy
the insatiable appetites of their
noisy young. Peak tourist season
begins in October; the heronries
can still be teeming with fledglings.

In winter this park is a haven
for waterfowl and raptors. Over
30 species of the latter, including
buzzards, eagles, hawks, falcons and
harriers, congregate here. Small
populations of the endangered
Siberian Crane can also be seen in
this season, although the numbers
have been steadily declining.

The habitats in Keoladeo range
from flourishing marshes to barren
tracts. They abound with mammals
and several reptiles such as pythons
and freshwater turtles. A solitary
tigress was sighted in 2001, but its
presence is a mystery as the park is
not connected to any known tiger
habitat. This is perhaps Bharatpur's
greatest attribute: you never know
what may turn up!

KEY SPECIES

MAMMALS Fishing Cat, Jungle Cat, Jackal,
Striped Hyena, Small Indian Civet,
Common Palm Civet, Common Mongoose,
Sambar, Spotted Deer (Chital), Nilgai (Blue
Bull), Blackbuck, Wild Boar, Indian
Porcupine, Smooth Indian Otter
REPTILES Common Monitor, Rock
Python, Flap-shell Turtle
BIRDS RAPTORS Pallas's Fish Eagle,
Greater Spotted Eagle, Short-toed Eagle,
Crested Serpent Eagle, Eurasian Marsh
Harrier, Dusky Eagle Owl, Brown Hawk
Owl, Peregrine Falcon
WOODLAND/SCRUB Grey Hornbill, Black-
rumped Flameback, White-bellied Drongo,
Rufous Treepie, Asian Paradise-flycatcher,
Bay-backed Shrike, Eurasian Thick-knee
WATERSIDE Siberian Crane, **Sarus Crane**
(*above*), Common Crane, Black-necked
Stork, Painted Stork, Asian Openbill,
Woolly-necked Stork, Eurasian Spoonbill,
Greater Flamingo, Darter, Great
Cormorant, Great White Pelican, Dalmatian
Pelican, Grey Heron, Purple Heron, Black-
crowned Night Heron, Black-headed Ibis,
Glossy Ibis, Purple Swamphen, Watercock,
Bar-headed Geese, Greylag Geese

Additional information on page 120

WESTERN ZONE

The western zone, much of it embraced by an extensive coastline, presents the many facets of India's wilderness. The colourful Thar or Great Indian Desert and the rare saline flatlands of the Rann of Kutch are habitats in incredible contrast to the rainy Konkan Coast and the biodiversity of the luxuriant Western Ghats. Parts of the western zone are densely populated and industrialized with conservation an uphill struggle, but the wildlife miraculously survives, some woefully on its last legs.

DESERT NATIONAL PARK

The Thar or Great Indian Desert lies predominantly in Rajasthan but spills over as salty flatlands and grassy sprawls into Gujarat's Kutch region. The world's most colourfully inhabited natural desert, it has at its heart the golden city of Jaisalmer, a popular tourist destination. The Desert National Park, an area of 3,162 sq km, is located 45 km west of this city.

Sand-dunes, both fixed and shifting, low rock-faces, grasslands and scrublands, characterize this park where the greatest need is for water. Vast tracts are encrusted with *sewan* grass, and the *aak* shrub and *khair*, *khejra* and *rohira* trees are widespread, but sand dominates every scene. Even so, many creatures have adapted to this harsh, inhospitable terrain. There are over 40 species of reptiles, including the burrowing Spiny-tailed Lizard, Russel's Viper, Saw-scaled Viper and the dragon-like Common Monitor. In a realm devoid of real fish, the Desert Skink is known as the sand-fish as it 'swims' or burrows through sand down to a depth of 30 cm. However, birds in their large numbers and variety are the most remarkable feature of this park. Nearly 120 species add colour to the dull shades of the desert.

The Indian Bustard and the wintering MacQueen's Bustard are highly endangered species that have benefited from the creation of the park. Flocks of sandgrouse arrive in winter from central Asia and can be seen at more or less fixed times in the morning at favoured waterholes. During

The park's sandy expanse, sparsely encrusted with grass and scrub, supports its unique wildlife.

this season, various waterfowl and flocks of migratory Demoiselle Crane are also seen near water. Larks, partridges, doves, bee-eaters, shrikes, chats, parakeets, babblers remain throughout the year, preyed upon by the buzzards, eagles, falcons and kites that hover and swoop over the landscape.

The Wolf burrows into sand-dunes to shelter from the daytime heat. Other predatory animals such as the Desert Fox, the Common Fox, the adaptable Jackal and the black-spotted Desert Cat are also shy and elusive but can be seen at waterholes. Desert Hare and the Long-eared Hedgehog are among the smaller denizens of the park. The strikingly beautiful Blackbuck, India's only true antelope, and the small but graceful Chinkara (Indian Gazelle) bound and leap amidst the sand-hills, sometimes surprisingly unafraid of humans. All forms of life gravitate towards water. The Sudasari waterhole is an excellent site for observing the animals. Observation hides also offer close encounters with desert wildlife.

Even this seemingly listless realm is beset by human demands, especially for water. It is the world's most populated desert but, as wildlife experts point out, the national park is a unique genetic storehouse of Indian desert wildlife and needs only the bare minimum to flourish. The ecology of the region would be disrupted with the artificial introduction of water.

KEY SPECIES

MAMMALS Blackbuck, Chinkara (Indian Gazelle), Nilgai (Blue Bull), Wolf, **Desert Fox** (*below*), Jackal, Desert Cat, Caracal, Desert Hare, Common Mongoose, Indian Desert Gerbil, Long-eared Hedgehog
REPTILES Spiny-tailed Lizard, Common Monitor, Sand Gecko, Russel's Viper
BIRDS BUSTARDS **Indian Bustard** (*above*), MacQueen's Bustard
RAPTORS Short-toed Eagle, Pallid Harrier, White-eyed Buzzard, Long-legged Buzzard, Tawny Eagle, Imperial Eagle, Steppe Eagle, Laggar Falcon, Cinereous Vulture, Short-eared Owl
SCRUB/OPEN AREAS Grey Francolin, Cream-coloured Courser, Indian Courser, Pin-tailed Sandgrouse, Black-bellied Sandgrouse, Chestnut-bellied Sandgrouse, Eurasian Thick-knee, Common Raven, Bimaculated Lark, Southern Grey Shrike, Stoliczka's Bushchat, Variable Wheatear, Desert Wheatear, Large Grey Babbler, Desert Warbler
WATERSIDE Demoiselle Crane, Common Crane, Black-winged Stilt

Additional information on page 121

WILD ASS (LITTLE RANN) WILDLIFE SANCTUARY

The sand-dunes of the Thar or Great Indian Desert slowly flatten out into a vast expanse of scrub-dotted, saline plain in the south. This is Gujarat's Rann of Kutch. The larger Great Rann to the north, abutting the Pakistan border and south Rajasthan, is renowned for its enormous breeding colony of flamingos. The Little Rann is the last stronghold of the Indian Wild Ass, or Ghorkhar, to which a 4953.71 sq km sanctuary has been dedicated. The Wild Ass Wildlife Sanctuary is also home to various other mammals such as the Nilgai, an antelope-like animal found only in India, the Wolf and the Indian Fox. A great assortment of birds can be sighted in winter. Cranes and flamingos gather in thousands; there are raptors in plenty and some rare MacQueen's Bustard.

It is said that Alexander the Great embarked on his journey home from a port in the Rann region when it was still an inlet of the sea. Gradually, the Rann was severed from the Gulf of Kutch. Dry and motorable between November and June, large tracts are still inundated by at least 30 cm of sea-water during the monsoon months. The Little Rann is only about 60 cm above sea-level, but over 70 *bets*, or patches of high ground, rise to almost 3 m. Pung Bet, the largest, spreads over 75 sq km. These less

The sociable Indian Wild Ass thrives on the saline sandy stretches of the Little Rann.

saline areas, with luxuriant grass cover interspersed with thorny scrub, are the mainstay of the Rann's flora and fauna, and of the wild ass in particular.

Once found across the drier tracts of north-west India and Pakistan, today the wild ass herds are confined to the Little Rann. E P Gee, the naturalist, estimated a population of barely 870 animals in 1962. Wild asses can run for long distances maintaining an average speed of about 50 km. Exploiting this fact, several tour operators take visitors on a wild ass chase across the desert, imperilling an already endangered animal. At dawn and dusk, the Little Rann is clothed in wonderful hues and it is a joy to view wild ass silhouettes against the setting sun. In the hot, dry months mirages are frequent, and blurred outlines of animals on quivering water can be seen one moment, uncannily disappearing the next.

The Indian Wild Ass has lived for long in relative harmony with its predominantly vegetarian human neighbours. Now the flourishing salt industry is jeopardizing the animal's future. Unfortunately, the Rann is perceived as a wasteland, which could be agriculturally developed by introducing adequate irrigational facilities. This would change its ecology irrevocably. Without proper protective measures, the wild ass's nimble-footedness may not be insurance enough against possible extinction.

KEY SPECIES

MAMMALS Indian Wild Ass, Blackbuck, Chinkara (Indian Gazelle), Nilgai (Blue Bull), Wolf, Caracal, Desert Cat, Indian Fox, Striped Hyena, Indian Pangolin, Small Indian Mongoose, Indian Desert Gerbil
REPTILES Spiny-tailed Lizard, Yellow Monitor, Black Cobra, Sand Boa
BIRDS BUSTARDS MacQueen's Bustard
RAPTORS Short-toed Snake Eagle, Long-legged Buzzard, Steppe Eagle, Imperial Eagle, Laggar Falcon, Saker Falcon, Short-eared Owl
SCRUB/OPEN AREAS Eurasian Thick-knee, Collared Pratincole, White-tailed Lapwing, **Yellow-wattled Lapwing** (*below*), Sirkeer Malkoha, Blue-cheeked Bee-eater, **Southern Grey Shrike** (*above*), Variable Wheatear, Common Stonechat
WATERSIDE Lesser Flamingo, Greater Flamingo, Asian Openbill, Woolly-necked Stork, White Stork, Eurasian Spoonbill, Great Crested Grebe, Great White Pelican, Dalmatian Pelican, Demoiselle Crane, Common Crane, Spotbill Duck, Gadwall, Northern Shoveler, Common Pochard, Tufted Duck, Caspian Tern, Pied Avocet

Additional information on page 121

MARINE NATIONAL PARK

A marine paradise teems with fantastic life-forms incredibly close to India's largest congregation of oil refineries near Jamnagar in Gujarat. The country's first marine reserve spreads along the south coast of the Gulf of Kutch for nearly 170 km and, together with its archipelago of 42 islands, sprawls over 163 sq km of intertidal zone.

The islands form a variegated cornucopia of colour and form. Coral reefs fringe 33 of them. The world here is like a large corporation, taking care of food, shelter, growth and security, and is marked by interdependent relationships between the various life-forms. Corals occur only on continental shelves that lie in warm, shallow and clear waters. The reefs are dominated by limestone shelters created by innumerable polyps, tiny soft-bodied marine animals. Extravagantly diverse in shape and size, and outrageously coloured, the reefs are a haven for myriad life-forms. In the Marine National Park, more than 200 species of molluscs have been identified along with as many of fish and nearly 60 of corals. Starfish, Brittle-stars, Sea-urchins, Sea-cucumbers and over 50 kinds of sponges are found in these waters, as are dolphins and the rare Sea-cow or Dugong. Sea-turtles are known to nest on the pristine beaches of several islands.

A wealth of marine species is supported by the mangrove-dominated ecosystem of the park.

Along the shoreline and numerous creeks are impregnable mangroves with nutrient-rich ooze that shelter a baffling array of life. Many fish species spend a part of their lives in these shallow waters while a multitude of birds find nesting and roosting sites amongst the mangroves. The park, especially around Beyt Dwarka, Okha and Pirotan Islands, is a paradise for birds. Strategically located along major avifaunal migration routes, it is blessed with a wide tidal range and nutrients. During winter, a legion of waders, such as flamingos, sandpipers, plovers and stints can be spotted in the park. Herons and terns and several other birds breed on the islands in summer. Boats are available for the keen bird-watcher.

James Hornell, the famous marine biologist who surveyed the region in 1905, remarked, "Never before in my life have I seen such a rich marine biota in so confined a place. It's God's own gift from heaven." In this fragile marine ecosystem, the fantastically attractive corals are a temptation to the casual visitor. The reefs are helpless against sedimentation and pollution. Over the past few years, refinery projects have burgeoned along the nearby coast and oil spills occur with unflinching regularity. Satellite data collected for 1975-85 indicates that sand-mining for cement has, in just a short decade, reduced the mangrove forests to half their extent.

KEY SPECIES

MAMMALS Dugong, Gangetic Dolphin, Jackal, Jungle Cat, Black-naped Hare

REPTILES Green Sea-turtle, Leatherback Turtle, Common Monitor

BIRDS RAPTORS White-tailed Eagle, Imperial Eagle, Steppe Eagle, Montagu's Harrier, Pallid Harrier, Black-shouldered Kite, Common Kestrel, Laggar Falcon, Peregrine Falcon

SCRUB/OPEN AREAS Grey Francolin, Indian Courser, Great Thick-knee, Rufous-tailed Shrike, Southern Grey Shrike, White-eared Bulbul, Variable Wheatear, Clamorous Reed Warbler

WATERSIDE Lesser Flamingo, Greater Flamingo, Crab-plover, Great Cormorant, Western Reef Egret, **Great White Pelican** (*above*), Dalmatian Pelican, White Stork, Demoiselle Crane, Common Crane, Pied Avocet, Eurasian Oystercatcher, Eurasian Curlew, Whimbrel, Black-tailed Godwit, Bar-tailed Godwit, Pacific Golden Plover, Ruddy Turnstone, Sanderling, Pallas's Gull, Yellow-legged Gull, Caspian Tern, Great Crested Tern

Additional information on page 122

BLACKBUCK (VELAVADAR) NATIONAL PARK

In the *bhal* or flat grasslands of Gujarat's Saurashtra peninsula, 65 km from Bhavnagar city, is the Blackbuck (Velavadar) National Park. It is amongst the last surviving stretches of relatively undisturbed grassland renowned for Blackbuck, Wolf and Lesser Florican. This 34.08 sq km area stretches between two seasonal rivers that drain into the Gulf of Cambay. Velavadar was declared a sanctuary in 1969, and upgraded to a national park in 1976.

Bhavnagar's royal family used this area as their private grazing lands and also as a hunting reserve. Blackbuck shared the alluvial plains with large herds of livestock, and were hunted down with the help of trained cheetahs. Post-independence, the gun, the plough and livestock ravaged the wilderness and with it the Blackbuck population. Once in the countless thousands, survival even in small isolated pockets became a challenge for this charming antelope. Velavadar was saved when local conservationists and the royal family stopped the practice of leasing out land for grazing and grass-cutting.

Numbering nearly 2,000 in the park, the shy Blackbuck are scattered across the endless waves of grass. The male's horns spiral to 60 cm in length. A legion of horns twisting above the swaying grass seems almost surreal, and to see them zipping across the plains in leaps and bounds,

Once highly persecuted, the Blackbuck has staged a remarkable recovery in Velavadar.

followed by a light-footed sprint, is an amazing experience. The Blackbuck is India's fastest ungulate and only true antelope. Everything about it is exquisite, even the sight of two rutting males preparing for combat, strutting with their heads held high, their splendid horns thrown back.

Blackbuck dominate the park, but there are several other mammals to see, such as Jackal and Jungle Cat. The Wolf just might oblige with a glimpse. Its sneaking ways have made it an animal held widely in suspicion, often falsely accused of lifting livestock when it prefers smaller prey. Its close relative, the Jackal, is much less secretive and known best for a howl that pierces eerily through the dark. There are many species of birds at Velavadar, including the rare Lesser Florican that comes at the onset of monsoon to breed. Raptors congregate in the winter. Harriers are low-flying raptors of open country that favour the *bhal* grasslands. The park is considered one of the largest harrier roosting sites in the world.

The involvement of the local people, especially the Kathi community, has played a critical role in safeguarding the Blackbuck and other wildlife in the park, although the antelope is often perceived as a usurper of fertile agricultural land. Misplaced notions need to be properly addressed or much conservation work may come to nought.

KEY SPECIES

MAMMALS Blackbuck, **Wolf** (*above*), Jackal, Jungle Cat, Common Indian Mongoose, **Nilgai (Blue Bull)** (*below*), Indian Desert Gerbil, Black-naped Hare, Wild Boar

BIRDS BUSTARDS Lesser Florican, MacQueen's Bustard

RAPTORS Pallid Harrier, Montagu's Harrier, Eurasian Marsh Harrier, Hen Harrier, Short-toed Eagle, Steppe Eagle, Imperial Eagle, Black-shouldered Kite, Laggar Falcon, Red-necked Falcon, Short-eared Owl

SCRUB/GRASS Grey Francolin, Rock Bush Quail, Savanna Nightjar, Indian Nightjar, Sirkeer Malkoha, Blue-cheeked Bee-eater, Southern Grey Shrike, Crested Lark, Rufous-tailed Lark, Rufous-tailed Shrike, Desert Wheatear, Variable Wheatear, Large Grey Babbler, Black-headed Bunting, Red-headed Bunting

WATERSIDE Sarus Crane, Demoiselle Crane, Common Crane, Painted Stork, Asian Openbill, Bar-tailed Godwit, Black-winged Stilt, White Stork

Additional information on page 122

GIR NATIONAL PARK

Until 200 years ago, the lion's habitat extended from south-east Europe, across south-west Asia to the northern part of central India. The Human population spread into this habitat and, coupled with indiscriminate hunting, sealed the fate of the Asian Lion. Unlike the tiger, the lion is easy game as it is active during the day and very sociable. Today, the last of the species, numbering less than 300, roam in the Gir forests of Gujarat, in an isolated hilly region of the otherwise flat Saurashtra peninsula. A sanctuary was created in 1965 and upgraded to a national park in 1975. After a famine in 1913, the lion population here reportedly dwindled to 20.

Lions, the star attraction of Gir, are accustomed to human beings and their vehicles, making close encounters possible. Leopards tend to be overlooked though they are seen occasionally hunting during the day. Jeep safaris to the Kankai and Kamleshwar reservoirs in the Chodavdi and Baval sectors of the park are the best way to observe deer, primates, Nilgai (Blue Bull) and Wild Boar. Gir is home to over 36 species of mammals, 450 of plants and 30 of reptiles, the most formidable being the Mugger (Marsh Crocodile). The park's topography makes it a bird-rich area with nearly 300 species that include woodland, scrubland and wetland varieties.

Intersected by rivers, Gir is a mix of low rocky hills and open areas, 42 km north of the coastal town of Veraval. It also encompasses reservoirs

The Gir National Park is the last stronghold of the Asian Lion, which number less than 300 here.

created by the damming of rivers such as the Hiran. Teak-dominated dry-deciduous forest covers much of the terrain but there is thorn-savannah vegetation in the park's eastern region. Ficus and other semi-evergreen trees grow here and there in the ravines.

The Asian Lion is under terrible pressure even in its last home. Continuous human movement and related activities are diminishing its already fragmented world. The Maldharis, pastoralists with a long history of living with the lion, occupy the 1153.42 sq km buffer area, about 2,200 of them living in *nesses*, or enclosed settlements, with almost 14,000 heads of livestock. Almost 10 km of the Visavadar-Veraval railway is routed through lion habitat, and there have been instances of lions and other animals being run over by trains. Two highways also run through Gir.

Confining the Asian Lion to a small area makes it vulnerable to biological, climatical and human-induced catastrophes. It is crucial that a second population be established. Several sites have been examined, but the translocation of a key predator requires an adequate prey base in a negligible human environment. In densely populated India, finding such a wilderness is difficult, although Palpur-Kuno Sanctuary in Madhya Pradesh is being considered as an option. For now, the Asian Lion roars only in the uneasy calm of Gir.

KEY SPECIES

MAMMALS Asian Lion (*above*), Leopard, Jungle Cat, Rusty-spotted Cat, Striped Hyena, Jackal, Indian Pangolin, Ratel, Spotted Deer (Chital), Sambar, Barking Deer, Blackbuck, Chowsingha (Four-horned Antelope), Nilgai (Blue Bull), Chinkara (Indian Gazelle), Wild Boar, Common Langur

REPTILES Mugger (Marsh Crocodile)

BIRDS RAPTORS Crested Serpent Eagle, Short-toed Eagle, Oriental Honey-buzzard, Shikra, Bonelli's Eagle, Booted Eagle, Osprey, Eurasian Eagle Owl

WOODLAND/SCRUB Indian Peafowl, Grey Francolin, Painted Francolin, Rock Bush Quail, Black-rumped Flameback, Indian Grey Hornbill, Yellow-footed Green Pigeon, Indian Roller, Plum-headed Parakeet, Sirkeer Malkoha, Pied Cuckoo, Asian Paradise-flycatcher, Indian Pitta, Rufous Treepie, Large Cuckooshrike, Jungle Myna

WATERSIDE Glossy Ibis, Darter, Painted Stork, Demoiselle Crane, Greylag Goose, Ruddy Shelduck, Spotbill Duck, Pied Kingfisher, White-browed Wagtail

Additional information on page 123

SANJAY GANDHI (BORIVLI) NATIONAL PARK

In a city of overwhelming contrasts, the Sanjay Gandhi National Park is a green oasis encircled by a wholly man-made landscape. It takes barely ten minutes to escape from the snarl of suburban Mumbai into this pristine wilderness, much of it protected since mid-1900s. Sandwiched between the western and the eastern suburbs, the park nestles in what is regarded as an outer spur of the Western Ghats. Elevation ranges from near sea-level at Bassein Creek, where the Ulhas River widens to join the sea, to nearly 500 m. Most of the park lies south of the creek.

The park embraces a wide range of habitats – dry, cactus-strewn rocky plateaus, miles of mixed-deciduous forest, pockets of semi–evergreen vegetation, the two sprawling reservoirs of Tulsi and Vihar, a mix of marshland and scrub, and a mangrove creek. It is hardly surprising that the region has a wealth of biodiversity that overshadows that of some of India's more reputed reserves. Rewarding nature walks can be enjoyed here even during peak monsoon months.

This park can be safely walked as there are no sizeable concentrations of the larger forms of wildlife. The area teems with over 150 species of butterflies, such as Blue Mormon and **Great Eggfly** (*facing page*).

The exotic gulmohur *tree blooms in summer in this predominantly mixed-deciduous forest.*

There are more than 800 species of flowering plants ranging from trees of red silk cotton, Indian laburnum and teak to shrubs such as the *karvi*, its purple blooms appearing only once every eight years.

Wild Boar, Black-naped Hare, small herds of Spotted Deer and Sambar, the occasional Jungle Cat and Common Palm Civet can be sighted in addition to various primates. The Leopard may be seen ambling along forest paths during early mornings and late evenings. Often in the news, it has claimed nearly 40 human lives since 1986. Crocodiles, pythons and several kinds of colourfully-patterned rock geckos are included in an inventory of over 50 reptilian forms.

Nearly 300 species of birds are the park's chief attraction. A three-hour walk in the winter months will introduce the visitor to at least 75 of them. Woodland birds include hornbills, Grey Junglefowl, Greater Racket-tailed Drongo and Emerald Dove. The lakes swarm with several waterbirds and raptors. The Malabar Pied Hornbill and the Great Hornbill were sighted here for the first time in February 2000.

The cave-riddled plateau of Kanheri presents a panoramic view of the city, the forest and the lakes. The park also has an extensive recreation zone. The wilderness area of the Sanjay Gandhi National Park exists wonderfully with development in Mumbai and is an ideal learning place for all.

KEY SPECIES

MAMMALS Leopard, Rusty-spotted Cat, Jungle Cat, Common Palm Civet, Sambar, Striped Hyena, Barking Deer, Spotted Deer (Chital), Common Langur, Bonnet Macaque, Rhesus Macaque, Wild Boar
REPTILES Mugger (Marsh Crocodile), Rock Python, Rock Gecko
BIRDS RAPTORS Crested Serpent Eagle, Shikra, Osprey, Peregrine Falcon, Lesser Spotted Eagle, Eurasian Marsh Harrier, White-bellied Sea Eagle, Eurasian Eagle Owl, Brown Hawk Owl
WOODLAND Grey Junglefowl, Red Spurfowl, Indian Peafowl, Painted Francolin, Greater Racket-tailed Drongo, Spangled Drongo, Bronzed Drongo, Ashy Drongo, Malabar Pied Hornbill, Great Hornbill, Indian Grey Hornbill, Emerald Dove, Malabar Trogon, **Black-hooded Oriole** (*above*), White-rumped Shama, Blue-capped Rock Thrush, Malabar Whistling Thrush, Crimson Sunbird
WATERSIDE Asian Openbill, Spotbill Duck, Lesser Whistling-duck, Oriental Dwarf Kingfisher, Pheasant-tailed Jacana

Additional information on page 123

DANDELI WILDLIFE SANCTUARY

The Dandeli Wildlife Sanctuary is one of the few nature reserves where, in addition to elephant and jeep rides in the forest, visitors can enjoy trekking on select routes. Covered with moist-deciduous forest, with pockets of tropical semi-evergreen and evergreen vegetation in its picturesque deep valleys, this is an ideal wilderness. The wildlife may be difficult to see, but the surroundings are unspoilt.

A ride in a coracle, a circular boat made of bamboo and covered with hide, is a pleasant way to explore the park. Meandering along the perennial Kali River and its tributaries, the Kaneri and the Nagajhari, animals such as the Gaur, mistakenly called the Indian Bison but actually a member of the ox family, and the Asian Elephant come into view on the banks. Turtles and crocodiles usually scamper away warily at the approach of a coracle. Plenty of birds can be seen, and Great Hornbills, Hill Mynas and Greater Racket-tailed Drongos keep up a constant chatter from within the dense forest. Tree-stumps jut out of water, perfect perches for cormorants and darters, whose widespread wings glisten in the sun.

The evergreen forest of Dandeli, on the spurs of the Western Ghats, is a vital corridor for wildlife.

The largely hilly Dandeli Wildlife Sanctuary lies on the spurs of the Western Ghats, the mountain range flanking India's west coast and known for its rich biodiversity. The sanctuary covers an 843.16 sq km area in Karnataka and is part of an almost contiguous forest, across north-west Karnataka, south-west Maharashtra and eastern Goa. Together with the Anshi National Park, the forests of Bhimgad and Radhanagri, and Goa's Cotigao and Netravali sanctuaries, this region forms a vital corridor for tigers and other wildlife.

Dandeli is of anthropological interest as well because of its resident tribal communities, which include the Gowlis and the Siddis. The former are nomadic graziers and the Siddis are believed to be the descendants of the African slaves who escaped from Portuguese custody nearly 400 years ago.

Several sites in and around the Dandeli Wildlife Sanctuary are worth a visit. The ancient limestone caves at Kavala and the monolithic granite formation of Syntheri Rock by the Kaneri River make for interesting trips. The crystal-clear spring waters at Mandurli and Kulagi, both within the sanctuary, are vital water sources. A trek to Siroli, the highest point in the Uttar Kannada district, affords a panoramic view of virgin forest. Another breathtaking view is of the wild and untamed Kali Valley from Sykes Point within the sanctuary.

KEY SPECIES

MAMMALS Asian Elephant, Tiger, Gaur (Indian Bison), Leopard, Wild Dog (Dhole), Sloth Bear, Malabar Giant Squirrel, Barking Deer, Mouse Deer, Common Palm Civet

BIRDS RAPTORS Crested Goshawk, Besra, Crested Serpent Eagle, Changeable Hawk Eagle, Brown Wood Owl, Brown Hawk Owl **WOODLAND/SCRUB** Grey Junglefowl, Indian Peafowl, Red Spurfowl, Great Hornbill, Malabar Pied Hornbill, Greater Racket-tailed Drongo, Spangled Drongo, Green Imperial Pigeon, Nilgiri Wood Pigeon, **Chestnut-headed Bee-eater** (*above*), Malabar Trogon, Hill Myna, Asian Fairy Bluebird, White-bellied Woodpecker, **White-cheeked Barbet** (*below*), Drongo Cuckoo, Malabar Parakeet, Ultramarine Flycatcher, Little Spiderhunter, Loten's Sunbird

Additional information on page 124

CENTRAL ZONE

Central India's stately sal forests, grassy meadows, shaded pools of water, tall feathery bamboo and vast animal herds inspired some of the most famous wildlife sagas and provided a setting for Rudyard Kipling's Jungle Book. Now it is home to India's most popular wildlife reserves. Dominated by the immense Deccan Plateau, this is a geologically ancient realm marked by low hills and extensive forests, grasslands, rivers and wetlands.

RANTHAMBORE TIGER RESERVE

Near the dusty town of Sawai Madhopur in Rajasthan is Ranthambore
Tiger Reserve, a forest often regarded as the world's finest for viewing
tigers and certainly the most documented. Conservation efforts have been
so successful here that the predator's habits changed from reclusive to
openly relaxed, often in the vicinity of human beings. The great cat can
sometimes be seen cooling off by day in a lake in the heat of summer or
ambling along a jungle track. Not infrequently, it hunts in broad daylight
and has been sighted charging a Sambar right into the lake waters.

It is sometimes possible to see the lordly tiger sauntering up the stairs
of the majestic ruin of the 10th-century Ranthambore Fort that looms
over the forest from a rocky outcrop. It was tossed back and forth through
centuries of war and confrontation, and was even the scene of a *jauhar*
(immolation by women to avoid dishonour). The forests around were once
the private hunting grounds of the Jaipur maharajas.

The 392 sq km Ranthambore National Park, the Kaila Devi Wildlife
Sanctuary and other small pockets of forest constitute the 1,334.64 sq km
Ranthambore Tiger Reserve. It lies towards the eastern limits of the
Aravali Range, close to where the Vindhya Range begins. Dry rocky crags
are networked by lakes and narrow rivulets, a majority of which are
waterless for much of the year. Dry deciduous forest of *dhok, ber* and *ronj*

Padam Talao is the largest of Ranthambore's lakes, and supports great numbers of wildlife.

dominates the park although semi-evergreen vegetation can be seen in some valleys and along the streams.

Bakaula, Lakarda, Nal Ghati, Semli, Anantpura and Kachida, popular areas for viewing wildlife in Ranthambore, are individually famous for their once-resident tigers, a few even immortalized in images and words. The lakes, Padam Talao, Raj Bagh and Milak Talao, are a magnet for wildlife and visitors. At the edge of Padam Talao stands the endearing red sandstone Jogi Mahal, and near it is an enormous banyan tree, which is proclaimed to be India's second-largest. Mugger (Marsh Crocodile) bask in the sun while herds of Nilgai (Blue Bull), Chinkara (Indian Gazelle), Sambar, Spotted Deer and troops of langur monkeys can be easily sighted. Leopard and Sloth Bear can also be seen, and jackals lurk by the lakes. Birds are represented by crowds of treepies, babblers, woodpeckers, parakeets, lapwings, partridges and the Indian Peafowl.

While the early years of Project Tiger clearly resulted in improved habitats and wildlife numbers, careful monitoring is a requisite for sustained conservation. This was more than amply demonstrated in Ranthambore by the tragic incidents of poaching in the early 1990s. Grazing of livestock, lack of adequate water and forest fires are some of the problems that the tiger reserve still faces.

KEY SPECIES

MAMMALS Tiger (*above*), Leopard, Jungle Cat, Striped Hyena, Jackal, Sloth Bear, Ratel, **Sambar** (*below*), Spotted Deer (Chital), Nilgai (Blue Bull), Chowsingha (Four-horned Antelope), Chinkara (Indian Gazelle), Common Langur, Wild Boar, Indian Pangolin, Small Indian Mongoose

BIRDS RAPTORS Crested Serpent Eagle, Bonelli's Eagle, Booted Eagle, Lesser Spotted Eagle, Pallas's Fish Eagle, Eurasian Eagle Owl, Brown Fish Owl, Collared Scops Owl

WOODLAND/SCRUB Indian Peafowl, Grey Francolin, Painted Spurfowl, Lesser Flameback, Rufous Treepie, Asian Paradise-flycatcher, White-bellied Minivet, Marshall's Iora, Indian Pitta, Large Grey Babbler, Common Woodshrike, White-bellied Drongo, Barred Buttonquail, Eurasian Thick-knee

WATERSIDE Painted Stork, Asian Openbill, Darter, Black-headed Ibis, Stork-billed Kingfisher, River Tern, Ruddy Shelduck, Pheasant-tailed Jacana, White-browed Wagtail, Great Thick-knee

Additional information on page 125

BANDHAVGARH TIGER RESERVE

The Bandhavgarh Tiger Reserve lies 300 km south-east of Khajuraho, famous worldwide for its erotic sculptures. The Vindhya hills, in which the reserve is located, are dotted with crucial wildlife parks. Bandhavgarh is one of the best managed, with local villagers included in forest-protection tasks. A popular wildlife destination, it can be crowded over the weekends.

According to local lore, Lord Rama, the epic hero of the *Ramayana*, stopped in these forests on his way back from Lanka, and in his entourage were two monkey architects responsible for the unique bridge spanning the waters between the mainland and Lanka. Legend says these 'architects' built the Bandhavgarh Fort, which Rama bequeathed to Lakshmana, his brother, venerated at a temple here as the *bandhavdhish* (lord of the fort).

Bandhavgarh was the private hunting estate of the Rewa maharajas. It is said that each maharaja killed the 'auspicious' number of 109 tigers, indicative of the big cat's population in this region in times past. Maharaja Martand Singh, however, was distressed by the state of the forest after years of uncontrolled poaching and offered it special protection in the early 1960s. The 105 sq km area was increased to include the adjoining forest tracts and in 1982 the area of the national park was recorded as 448.84 sq km.

The rugged terrain is dominated by a high plateau punctuated by wildlife-rich grassy sprawls, originally marshlands designed to protect the fort. Some of the swampy areas still

Marshy areas amid towering sal forests (above) *largely constitute the reserve, where the Indian Roller* (left) *can be often seen.*

exist amid towering sal forests and contrasting tracts of bamboo. This deciduous setting, drained by numerous streams, is an ideal tiger habitat. The 1997 census reported 44 tigers, and visitors are often rewarded with fairly clear views of this elusive cat. It was in these forests near Rewa that a white tiger was last seen in the wild and captured in 1957. Since then, no more sightings of white tigers have been reported. White tigers are not a separate species, but a strain of albinism gives them a pale coat. All Bandhavgarh tigers today exhibit normal colouring.

Walking is prohibited but guided elephant and jeep rides to Khilouli and Sehra Dadra, classic grazing grounds in the reserve, provide interesting insights into the Indian jungle and offer plenty of wildlife to view. Winter is the best time for bird-watching. Over 200 species include the Red Junglefowl and the Malabar Pied Hornbill.

Bandhavgarh is wonderfully geared for tourism with a broad network of well-maintained roads and comfortable accommodation. The forest department's holistic approach ensures that this reserve is run well and wisely. In order to get a panoramic view of the surrounding landscape, so integral to India and immortalized by Rudyard Kipling in *The Jungle Book*, a visit to the historic fort of Bandhavgarh is a necessary and an unforgettable experience.

KEY SPECIES

MAMMALS Tiger (*above*), Leopard, Wild Dog (Dhole), Jungle Cat, Common Palm Civet, Jackal, Striped Hyena, Sloth Bear, Gaur (Indian Bison), Sambar, Spotted Deer (Chital), Barking Deer, Mouse Deer, Chowsingha (Four-horned Antelope), Chinkara (Indian Gazelle), Nilgai (Blue Bull), Indian Pangolin, Ratel, Common Mongoose, Common Langur

BIRDS RAPTORS Crested Serpent Eagle, Changeable Hawk Eagle, Oriental Honey-buzzard, Shikra, Common Kestrel, Mottled Wood Owl, Dusky Eagle Owl

WOODLAND/SCRUB Red Junglefowl, Painted Francolin, Grey Francolin, Painted Spurfowl, Malabar Pied Hornbill, Streak-throated Woodpecker, White-naped Woodpecker, Lesser Yellownape, Greater Racket-tailed Drongo, Indian Roller, Drongo Cuckoo, Indian Pitta, Large Cuckooshrike, Black-headed Cuckooshrike, Black-hooded Oriole, Tickell's Blue Flycatcher, Blue Rock Thrush, Orange-headed Thrush

WATERSIDE Painted Stork, Black-headed Ibis, Grey Heron, Lesser Whistling-duck, Black-winged Stilt, Stork-billed Kingfisher

Additional information on page 126

PALAMAU TIGER RESERVE

A series of highlands dominate peninsular India's topography, one of them being the extensive Chota Nagpur Plateau. This was once a wilderness teeming with wildlife, including the ill-fated cheetah, now found only in Africa. District gazetteers of the late 19th century recorded the monetary rewards for eliminating 'pest' animals: Rs 25 for a tiger and Rs 5 for a leopard. The Betla forests on the Chota Nagpur Plateau were much sought after by big game hunters until the Betla National Park was established. This and the larger Palamau Wildlife Sanctuary to the south constitute the Palamau Tiger Reserve, which is over 1,000 sq km in extent and lies within the state of Jharkhand, north-west of the industrial city of Ranchi.

The meandering North Koel River and its tributary, the Auranga, cut through the rugged landscape of Palamau's northern section. The Kanhar and Amanat rivers flow through the Betla section of the tiger reserve area amidst majestic stands of sal and other dry-deciduous trees. The fruit of the *bael* tree and *mohwa* flowers are enjoyed by the resident herbivores. Dry and parched during summer, the forests are rejuvenated in the monsoon when the rivers overflow. Low waterfalls suddenly appear and make Palamau Tiger Reserve a pleasant place to visit in the rainy season.

However, for sheer numbers of animals, the hot, dry summer months are ideal when animals are drawn to water and can be often sighted. The Hathibajwa watch-tower and the observation hide at Madhuchuan in the

Palamau is one of the foremost tiger reserves, but the great cat is not very easy to sight here today.

Betla area overlook waterholes, popular with wildlife. Several steps have been taken to improve the water situation here. The deepening of natural springs, the creation of artificial waterholes and habitat protection are yielding results.

Palamau was once the seat of the Gond Chero rajas who were responsible for the imposing 16th-century forts on the banks of the Koel and the Auranga. Thick, virgin forest formed an almost impregnable shield from Daud Khan's invading army in 1660, and through much of the late 19th and early 20th centuries these forests served as royal hunting grounds.

In India, the first-ever tiger census based on pugmark count was taken in Palamau in 1934. Wild elephants can be sighted here, sometimes cooling off in the waters of the Betla storage dam. Their numbers are small and it is believed that they were introduced to this region. The Maharaja of Surguja may have released about 20 elephants to establish a population here, but it is possible that the great beasts migrated from surrounding forests in the early 1900s.

Industrialization is considered an antidote for all ills in the newly-carved state of Jharkhand, exerting tremendous pressure on wilderness areas. Palamau was amongst the first nine reserves of Project Tiger started in 1973, but now it requires tremendous efforts to ensure long-lasting, continued conservation.

KEY SPECIES

MAMMALS Tiger, Asian Elephant, Leopard, Wild Dog (Dhole), Jungle Cat, Wolf, Small Indian Civet, Jackal, Striped Hyena, **Sloth Bear** (*below*), Gaur (Indian Bison), Sambar, Spotted Deer (Chital), Barking Deer, Indian Pangolin, **Common Langur** (*above*)

BIRDS RAPTORS Crested Serpent Eagle, Lesser Spotted Eagle, Steppe Eagle, Grey-headed Fish Eagle, White-eyed Buzzard, Common Kestrel, Eurasian Eagle Owl

WOODLAND/SCRUB Red Junglefowl, Black Francolin, Oriental Pied Hornbill, Greater Flameback, Green-billed Malkoha, Grey-bellied Cuckoo, Greater Racket-tailed Drongo, Indian Pitta, Black-hooded Oriole, Jungle Myna, Asian Paradise-flycatcher, White-rumped Shama

WATERSIDE Lesser Adjutant, Black Stork, Woolly-necked Stork, Painted Stork, Grey Heron, Black Ibis, Stork-billed Kingfisher

Additional information on page 127

KANHA TIGER RESERVE

The Kanha Tiger Reserve offers pristine habitats for a wide variety of wildlife. Research and proper management has increased the wildlife population and enhanced the habitat for some species. Although walking and night visits are prohibited, the ease with which large numbers of animals can be spotted has made this amongst the finest and most important wildlife sites in India. The reserve is closed between July and October, but premature showers could result in its earlier closure.

Kanha is celebrated for its valleys with their towering forests and famous grasslands, or *maidans*. An imposing army of herbivores can always be seen on the *maidans*, with the Spotted Deer easily outnumbering the rest. *Dadars* or large grass- and scrub-encrusted plateaus on the Maikal Hills, ranging in altitude from 450 to 900 m, are ideal Gaur habitat. The rocky cliff-like ridges edging the plateaus overlook the park's spectacular landscape. The slopes, carved by myriad *nullahs* or ravines, are covered by mixed forest and plenty of dense bamboo, climbers and undergrowth, perfect for the reclusive Tiger.

For the bird enthusiast, jeep rides and elephant safaris can be very rewarding. A day's count can be as high as 120 species, especially during the winter months. Wildfowl, hornbills, eagles, woodpeckers, drongos and

The central Indian Barasingha can often be sighted in Kanha's large, grassy clearings.

scores of other woodland birds keep the tally going. Shravan Tal, located in the central meadows of Kanha, is an unforgettable site for the avid bird-watcher.

Another memorable experience in Kanha is tracking tigers on elephant-back. The *mahout* is not only the elephant trainer and driver, but an incredible forest guide and philosopher. He possesses an uncanny knack for locating the tiger by being ever alert to the warning cries of monkeys and deer, and to the majestic cat's distinctive excreta, pug-marks on the ground and claw-marks on tree trunks.

The valleys of Kanha were the hunting grounds of the rich and powerful, with the tiger as the foremost attraction. The central Indian Barasingha, a race of Swamp Deer of which there was a sizeable population 100 years ago, was also hunted down. In 1933, realizing the region's wildlife potential, 250 sq km of the Kanha Valley was offered protection, followed by the adjoining Halon Valley a couple of years later. However, the indiscriminate killing continued until, ironically, the massacre of several tigers by a privileged hunter caused such an uproar that a special legislation was passed that finally saved Kanha for posterity. It is today a 1,945 sq km Project Tiger reserve, a move that has not only helped the Tiger survive, but very successfully saved the Swamp Deer in central India.

KEY SPECIES

MAMMALS Tiger (*below*), **Swamp Deer (Barasingha)** (*above*), Leopard, Wild Dog (Dhole), Leopard-cat, Jungle Cat, Indian Fox, Sloth Bear, Gaur (Indian Bison), Sambar, Spotted Deer (Chital), Barking Deer, Chowsingha (Four-horned Antelope), Nilgai (Blue Bull), Blackbuck, Indian Pangolin, Ratel, Common Mongoose
BIRDS RAPTORS Bonelli's Eagle, Changeable Hawk Eagle, Booted Eagle, Oriental Honey-buzzard, Crested Serpent Eagle, Brown Fish Owl, Jungle Owlet
WOODLAND/SCRUB Red Junglefowl, Painted Spurfowl, Painted Francolin, Indian Peafowl, Malabar Pied Hornbill, Streak-throated Woodpecker, Lesser Yellownape, Heart-spotted Woodpecker, Emerald Dove, Banded Bay Cuckoo, Indian Cuckoo, Indian Pitta, Spangled Drongo, Greater Racket-tailed Drongo, Large Cuckooshrike, Black-hooded Oriole, Orange-headed Thrush
WATERSIDE Black Ibis, Woolly-necked Stork, Lesser Adjutant, Painted Stork, Stork-billed Kingfisher

Additional information on page 127

NAGZIRA WILDLIFE SANCTUARY & NAWEGAON NATIONAL PARK

Nagzira Wildlife Sanctuary, 120 km to the north-east of Nagpur, is in the Gondia district in eastern Maharashtra, and nearby is its twin wilderness, the Nawegaon National Park. Both are south of the Satpura Hills, in a critically viable habitat for tiger, gaur and many other species. An unusual animal is the Indian Pangolin, its armour of protective scales giving it a peculiar appearance. Elusive and overlooked due to its largely nocturnal prowls, the pangolin is superbly modified to feed off ants and termites.

An excellent network of forest trails leads to splendid wildlife-viewing spots, such as the watch-towers around the small Nagzira Lake in the centre of the sanctuary. The trail that leads to Mangezari in the extreme north passes by the observation hide at Bandarchuwa and some rewarding stretches of forest. A drive around the lake to Murpar and another west, towards Wakdabehada and Andharban offers plenty of opportunities for observing wildlife. Gaur, Sloth Bear, Sambar, Spotted Deer and the occasional Leopard can be sighted. Nearly all water-bodies dry up in the heat of summer, but the lake and a few waterholes sustain the animals.

In marked contrast, the Nawegaon National Park, 45 km south of Nagzira, is dotted with perennial lakes. The largest in this forested

The Little Egret is one of many waterbirds often sighted near the water-bodies of Nawegaon.

landscape is the Nawegaon Lake, nearly 11 sq km in extent, with Maldongri, a small island, in the middle. Kolu Patel Kohli is said to have created this lake in the early 18th century. A shrine in his memory is built on one of the low hills around the lake. Amongst the more prominent of the smaller lakes is Itiadoh.

Lying in the low Nishani Hills and less undulating than Nagzira, Nawegaon is covered mostly by mixed-deciduous forest. The lakes attract herbivores and predators alike, and are a major draw for human visitors too. The birds at Nawegaon provide a special thrill. The park has a mix of forest and aquatic habitats which attract an amazing number of species. Almost half the bird species recorded in Maharashtra have been spotted in this 134 sq km area.

The relatively easy sightings of several animal species, excellent jungle roads, which often skirt the lake, well-located watch-towers and waterholes, and the simple but clean accommodation have made this park a popular destination for nature enthusiasts. However, there is a fear that its easy accessibility may encourage the casual visitor and cause a degeneration of the sites into mere picnic spots. On the other hand, with efficient management, the park could create a greater awareness and generate much-required goodwill for the cause of nature conservation.

KEY SPECIES

MAMMALS Tiger, **Leopard** (*above*), Wild Dog (Dhole), Jungle Cat, Common Palm Civet, Jackal, Striped Hyena, Sloth Bear, Gaur (Indian Bison), Sambar, Spotted Deer (Chital), Barking Deer, Mouse Deer, Chowsingha (Four-horned Antelope), Chinkara (Indian Gazelle), Nilgai (Blue Bull), Indian Pangolin
BIRDS RAPTORS Crested Serpent Eagle, Changeable Hawk Eagle, Grey-headed Fish Eagle, Osprey, Eurasian Marsh Harrier, Black-shouldered Kite, Oriental Honey-buzzard, White-eyed Buzzard, Common Kestrel, Red-necked Falcon, Brown Fish Owl, Mottled Wood Owl
WOODLAND/SCRUB Grey Junglefowl, Painted Spurfowl, Painted Francolin, Emerald Dove, White-naped Woodpecker, Indian Pitta, Greater Racket-tailed Drongo, Large Cuckooshrike, Black-hooded Oriole, Scarlet Minivet
WATERSIDE Sarus Crane, Painted Stork, Asian Openbill, Black Ibis, Grey Heron, Great Cormorant, Darter, Indian Cormorant, Comb Duck, Spotbill Duck, Eurasian Wigeon, Lesser Whistling-duck, Northern Shoveler, Pintail

Additional information on page 128

TADOBA-ANDHARI TIGER RESERVE

Chandrapur is an industrial town in the Deccan heartland of eastern Maharashtra, a region otherwise poorly developed. Between the 14th and 16th centuries, the Gonds (a pre-Aryan people) ruled the vast forested tracts, with Chandrapur (or Chanda as it was then known) as their capital. The Mughal emperor, Akbar, captured the territories of the Gond in the 16th century and the Marathas annexed this kingdom not long after. In the early years of British rule, it was an immense, thickly forested expanse teeming with wild game and numerous rivers. F C Hicks, a British officer posted at Chanda recorded as late as in 1911 that he had been "cut off from all intercourse with civilization and railways by hundreds of miles of almost impenetrable forests, swollen rivers and malarious marshes."

Minor restrictions were imposed on the area in the early 1900s to preserve it as a prime hunting location. However, hunting itself was banned only in 1935. In 1955, an area of 116.54 sq km was declared the Tadoba National Park, and when it was transferred to Maharashtra the following year, it became the state's first national park. In early 1986, an adjacent tract of 508.85 sq km was declared the Andhari Wildlife Sanctuary. Together, these formed the Tadoba-Andhari Tiger Reserve

The elusive Leopard can sometimes be encountered in broad daylight in Tadoba's deciduous forests.

in 1993, a viable area for wildlife, especially tiger and gaur.

Tadoba is a mix of rugged terrain and open meadows, with the Tadoba Lake in the north. Motorable paths radiating from the lake are fairly well laid out for viewing wildlife in the various parts of the park. Salt-licks and waterholes, such as the Panchdhara and Pandharpauni, are sites of much animal activity. There are several *machans*, or observation hides, but the two at the lake make for the most interesting experiences as the water-body is a magnet for Tadoba's wildlife. Katezari in the core zone of the park is another rewarding spot as is Jamunbodi with its mix of grassland and thick deciduous forest. Teak occurs abundantly amongst *mohwa*, *jamun* and mango trees and clumps of bamboo. The trees are home to a host of langur monkeys, and the fruits and leaves they shake off the branches attract Spotted Deer. The lake and the backwaters of the Erai dam host a healthy number of winter waterfowl and raptors, adding to Tadoba's impressive avifauna.

Moharli, at the main gate of the reserve, is the chosen site for a tourist complex. Regarded by many as Maharashtra's best-managed wildlife areas, nature rules at Tadoba-Andhari, but the reserve needs safeguards against the expanding industrial and mining neighbourhood before it becomes a serious threat.

KEY SPECIES

MAMMALS Tiger, Leopard, Wild Dog (Dhole), Jungle Cat, Sloth Bear, **Gaur (Indian Bison)** (*below*), Spotted Deer (Chital), **Sambar** (*above*), Common Palm Civet, Small Indian Civet, Wild Boar, Nilgai (Blue Bull), Chowsingha (Four-horned Antelope), Barking Deer, Ratel, Indian Pangolin, Common Langur
REPTILES Mugger (Marsh Crocodile)
BIRDS RAPTORS Crested Serpent Eagle, Changeable Hawk Eagle, Oriental Honey-buzzard, Shikra, Grey-headed Fish Eagle, Common Kestrel, Mottled Wood Owl, Brown Fish Owl
WOODLAND/SCRUB Grey Junglefowl, Red Spurfowl, Painted Francolin, Greater Racket-tailed Drongo, Indian Pitta, Scarlet Minivet, Large Cuckooshrike, Emerald Dove, Oriental Turtle Dove, Indian Scimitar Babbler, Black-hooded Oriole, Orange-headed Thrush, White-rumped Shama
WATERSIDE Painted Stork, Asian Openbill, Grey Heron, Black-headed Ibis, Stork-billed Kingfisher, Pheasant-tailed Jacana

Additional information on page 128

PENCH TIGER RESERVE

Central India once presented an almost contiguous realm for tigers, and even now, despite extensive deforestation and human settlement, seven of India's 27 tiger reserves are located here. Maharashtra and Madhya Pradesh share the Pench Tiger Reserve in the southern, lower reaches of the Satpura Hills, less than 90 km north of Nagpur city. In Madhya Pradesh, the reserve is nearly 758 sq km, while the Maharashtra area is 257 sq km. Although a contiguous tiger habitat, and together declared as the country's 19th tiger reserve in 1992, the two areas are administered separately.

The reserve gets its name from the Pench River. Characterized by a low, hilly landscape covered with mixed-deciduous forest, the region has some old teak plantations and roughly marks the northern limit of this tree. Bamboo stands add to the charm of the setting. Although there are several perennial pools, many rivulets dry up in summer. Together with the many smaller streams, they form a perfect environment for tigers.

Towards the southern margins of Madhya Pradesh's Pench Tiger Reserve, the reservoir created by the Totladoh hydroelectric project

In the vast forested tracts of the Pench Tiger Reserve, small herds of Gaur are a frequent sight.

covers, at maximum capacity, well over 65 sq km of rich natural habitat. However, over time the water-body has become a major draw for wildlife, including the waterbirds, seen in profusion during winter. The region has more than 200 species of birds, and the months from December to March are ideal for a visit.

An excellent network of jungle trails and roads ensure easy access to the tourist zones. Herds of Spotted Deer and the majestic Sambar are common in clearings, by the roadside and near the reservoir or the river. The small-built Barking Deer (Muntjac) enjoy the thick forests. From a distance their call could be mistaken for the barking of a dog. Other animals such as gaur, jackal and wild boar can also be seen.

Pench Tiger Reserve is easily accessible by road, Nagpur-Jabalpur highway (NH-7) passing so close to the reserve that it has been suspected of disturbing the wildlife in the area. The Gonds are Pench's most prominent tribe. Their mostly agricultural, tribal lifestyles are intimately associated with the forest and it is imperative that conservation does not harm their interests. The India Eco-development Project, started here in 1996-97, helps villagers develop their own resources, reduce dependency on the forest and understand, accept and participate in the objectives of Project Tiger.

KEY SPECIES

MAMMALS Tiger, Leopard, Wild Dog (Dhole), Jungle Cat, Common Indian Civet, Jackal, Striped Hyena, Sloth Bear, Gaur (Indian Bison), Sambar, Spotted Deer (Chital), Barking Deer, Nilgai (Blue Bull), Chowsingha (Four-horned Antelope), Indian Pangolin, **Common Langur** (*below*)
BIRDS **RAPTORS** **Crested Serpent Eagle** (*above*), Bonelli's Eagle, Changeable Hawk Eagle, Oriental Honey-buzzard, White-eyed Buzzard, Mottled Wood Owl, Jungle Owlet **WOODLAND/SCRUB** Grey Junglefowl, Painted Spurfowl, Painted Francolin, Indian Peafowl, Emerald Dove, Brown-headed Barbet, Streak-throated Woodpecker, White-naped Woodpecker, Spotted Creeper, Grey-bellied Cuckoo, Indian Cuckoo, Greater Racket-tailed Drongo, Black-hooded Oriole, Eurasian Golden Oriole, Scarlet Minivet, Asian Paradise-flycatcher **WATERSIDE** Painted Stork, Black-headed Ibis, Grey Heron, Great Thick-knee, Stork-billed Kingfisher

Additional information on page 129

MELGHAT TIGER RESERVE

The forests of the Satpura Hills in the 1900s were "as much like an earthly paradise as anything can be in this unsatisfactory world", according to R G Burton's *Sport and Wildlife in the Deccan*. The Melghat Tiger Reserve is situated in these forests amidst the Gawilgarh Hills, a south-west branch of the Satpuras. Over the centuries, invaders infiltrated into central India through passes in these rugged hills. In 1484, the Imad Shahi dynasty was founded at the impressive hilltop fortress of Gawilgarh, close to the southeast fringes of Melghat. Another fort at Narnala added to their glory.

Melghat, which translates to 'a meeting of hills', encompasses the Gugamal National Park. Mountain spurs are interconnected by plateaus, while ravines, or *khoras*, cut through the hills. Bairat, Chilati and Bhoot

Khoras are known for their natural beauty. The pleasant little hill town of Chikhaldara, established in colonial times, lies atop Vairat (1,178 m), just outside the reserve. Melghat itself has dry-deciduous forests of teak and bamboo, with

The Sipna River (above) *flows through Melghat, where the Leopard* (left) *is a key predator.*

a smattering of semi-evergreen trees along the stream-beds.

The forests of Melghat are a crucial catchment area for the large, drought-prone expanse of central India. The Tapti River forms the reserve's northern boundary and a network of streams runs through its craggy landscape. Over the years, habitat protection has raised the groundwater level, waterholes have been dug and small earthen dams have been built to impound water for the long, dry summer months.

Hot as it is, summer is also the time when Melghat's wildlife is easier to sight as the undergrowth is scanty. Scattered herds of Gaur are a common sight. Referred to as the Indian Bison, this massive ox is essentially a hill animal, although it frequently descends in its quest for pasture. Several other herbivores are also seen here. Tigers are elusive, but a meeting with a Leopard or a Sloth Bear is probable. Grey Junglefowl and other woodland birds abound in the park. Towards late May, the whistling cry of the Indian Pitta resounds across the scorched forest. Visits to Koktoo and Semadoh, prime Gaur and Tiger habitats, offer the best opportunities for wildlife viewing.

In keeping with most other protected areas in India, Melghat too is trapped in a multitude of troubles: the threat of forest fires, water scarcity and an unwelcome interest in the wilderness for timber and developmental projects.

KEY SPECIES

MAMMALS Tiger, Leopard, Wild Dog (Dhole), Jungle Cat, Common Palm Civet, Jackal, Striped Hyena, Sloth Bear, Gaur (Indian Bison), **Sambar** (*above*), Spotted Deer (Chital), Barking Deer, Mouse Deer, Chowsingha (Four-horned Antelope), Nilgai (Blue Bull), Indian Pangolin, Indian Porcupine

BIRDS RAPTORS Crested Serpent Eagle, Oriental Honey-buzzard, Eurasian Hobby, Bonelli's Eagle, Mottled Wood Owl, Jungle Owlet

WOODLAND/SCRUB Grey Junglefowl, Indian Peafowl, Grey Francolin, Painted Francolin, Red Spurfowl, Greater Racket-tailed Drongo, White-bellied Drongo, Indian Grey Hornbill, White-naped Woodpecker, Chestnut-bellied Nuthatch, Indian Pitta, Emerald Dove, Oriental Turtle Dove, Sirkeer Malkoha, Malabar Whistling Thrush, Orange-headed Thrush, Indian Scimitar Babbler, Black-hooded Oriole, Large Cuckooshrike, Scarlet Minivet, Verditer Flycatcher, Asian Paradise-flycatcher, Crested Bunting

Additional information on page 129

EASTERN ZONE

A region of immense biodiversity, India's enchanting east hosts many of the country's rare and endangered mammals, over 8,000 species of plants and nearly 600 of birds. The zone is famous for the Sunderbans, the world's largest estuarine mangrove forest, for the 8,585 m high Khangchendzonga, the third tallest mountain peak in the world, and for Cherrapunji in Meghalaya, until recently proclaimed as the planet's wettest spot. The mighty Brahmaputra River flows through this zone, flooding and wreaking havoc every year, and with a stupendous influence on the region's wildlife.

Namdapha Tiger Reserve

The dark evergreen forests of Namdapha Tiger Reserve in Arunachal Pradesh are a maze of enormous trees, lavish epiphytes and ferns, and serpent-like creepers. A land of rich biodiversity, it rings with the cry of the Hoolock, the only ape in India, and the clamour of countless birds.

The altitudinal range of the reserve is immense, from a low of 200 m to the 4,598 m Dapha Bum peak in the north, and embraces a prodigious mix of habitats – moist bamboo forests, dense, wet evergreen jungles, moist temperate and alpine scrublands. More than 90 per cent of the 1,985 sq km tiger reserve has been retained as a core zone.

Much of Namdapha remains wild and unspoiled. Only one road passes through the reserve's southern half and then through the buffer area, in the western-central part, to connect Miao to the nearby Myanmar border. This road, often routed close by the Noa-Dehing River, was largely constructed long before Namdapha was declared a tiger reserve.

Lying in the Noa-Dehing catchment area that opens westward into the Upper Brahmaputra Valley, Namdapha is mostly snow-free. A national park had been suggested in the 1940s, the area then a part of the North East

Drained by innumerable rivers, Namdapha's tropical forest is a vast storehouse of flora and fauna.

Frontier Agency (NEFA), but the
reserve came into being only under
the Assam Forest Regulation of
1970. It was later accorded the
status of a wildlife sanctuary, and
upgraded to a national park in
1983, when it was also included
in Project Tiger.

Some of India's most elusive
wildlife, the thick-set goat-antelope
called the Mishmi Takin, the
Binturong or Bear-cat, the Red
Panda, known also as the Cat-bear,
the Golden Cat and the Marbled
Cat, all live in this reserve.
Namdapha is unusual in that it
hosts four species of large cats –
Tiger, Clouded Leopard, Leopard
and Snow Leopard. There is a
wealth of other mammals (at least
70 species), which includes several
of the lesser cats, plenty of squirrels
and primates such as the Hoolock
or White-browed Gibbon.

As for birds, this is one of the
richest areas in India, with over
400 species of mostly woodland
varieties. Forest trails offer good
sightings. The several natural lakes
(or *bils*) and smaller pools attract
winter migratory birds as well as
resident waterbirds, a category that
includes the endangered White-
winged Duck. Little is known of
the thousands of other life-forms
that inhabit this tropical paradise.
In view of its unique importance,
Namdapha deserves special
attention before the juggernaut of
development takes over one of
India's last wild frontiers.

KEY SPECIES

MAMMALS Tiger, Clouded Leopard, Snow
Leopard (Ounce), Binturong, Leopard-cat,
Marbled Cat, Golden Cat, Mishmi Takin,
Wild Dog (Dhole), **Red Panda** (*above*),
Large Indian Civet, Himalayan Palm Civet,
Gaur (Indian Bison), Goral, Musk Deer,
Slow Loris, Serow, Hoolock Gibbon,
Assamese Macaque, Capped Langur,
Himalayan Weasel, Hog Badger, Sambar
BIRDS RAPTORS Lesser Fish Eagle,
Mountain Hawk Eagle, Rufous-bellied
Eagle, Pied Falconet, Oriental Hobby,
Crested Serpent Eagle, Crested Goshawk
WOODLAND/SCRUB Blyth's Tragopan,
Rufous-throated Partridge, Red Junglefowl,
Grey Peacock Pheasant, Great Hornbill,
Rufous-necked Hornbill, Wreathed
Hornbill, Great Slaty Woodpecker, Bay
Woodpecker, Greater Yellownape, Golden-
throated Barbet, Ward's Trogon, Dollarbird,
Green Cochoa, Chestnut-winged Cuckoo,
Mountain Imperial Pigeon, Collared
Treepie, Rufous-vented Laughingthrush,
Greater Rufous-headed Parrotbill,
Large Niltava, Whiskered Yuhina, Grey-
headed Parrotbill
WATERSIDE White-winged Duck, Ibisbill,
White-bellied Heron, Slaty-backed Forktail,
White-crowned Forktail, Crested
Kingfisher, Brown Dipper

Additional information on page 130

KAZIRANGA NATIONAL PARK

On the swampy southern banks of the Brahmaputra River lies the
Kaziranga National Park, an absolute contrast to the dense forests of
Manas Tiger Reserve to the north. Kaziranga's ecology is dominated by
the river, which floods dramatically every year. A tributary, the Moru
Diphlu, forms the park's southern boundary and exacerbates the flood
situation. As much as three-quarters of the park may get submerged.
Animals are forced to higher grounds, but hundreds still perish every year.
Post-monsoon, Kaziranga transforms into a swamp thriving with wildlife.

A World Heritage Site in Assam, Kaziranga constitutes miles of shallow
swamp and tall elephant grass with dense forest. The Mikir Hills to its
south-west rise to nearly 1,220 m and some of the rivulets that flow down
from these hills drain into the many lakes (*bils*) within the park.

Kaziranga has the largest population of the One-horned Rhinoceros,
over 1,200 individuals at last count. In the 1800s, the area was the hunting
preserve of the local rajas, one of whom is said to have killed 97 rhinos in
a month! Such mindless slaughter almost wiped out the species, and by
1908 the surviving population was estimated at only 12. Stringent steps
were then taken and in 1926, the area was offered protection. It remained
closed to the public until 1938. Kaziranga received the status of a

Kaziranga's swamps host the world's largest surviving population of the One-horned Rhinoceros.

sanctuary in 1940 but it was only in 1954, when the Assam Rhino Bill was passed, that the animal finally received the special protection it needed. Kaziranga became a national park in 1974. Most of the park's wildlife can be easily seen, often in a couple of days. Though the forest department organizes mini-bus and jeep rides, the unhurried elephant rides are the most rewarding, facilitating close encounters with Swamp Deer (Barasingha), Hog-deer, Asian Elephant, and of course, the One-horned Rhinoceros. Tigers are rarely sighted in the maze of elephant grass and dense growth. The avifauna is extremely rich and varied, and includes both waterside and woodland birds.

This wealth of species makes Kaziranga a highly visited reserve in the flood-free months and the park can get especially crowded over weekends. Bordered by human settlements and tea plantations, it is a troubled wilderness, and for a while faced the brunt of social unrest. To escape the flood waters the wildlife often moves outside the park, where it is more exposed to poachers. Conservation initiatives to increase the park's area to 820 sq km from the present 472 sq km are in progress, though slow-moving.

Meanwhile, life continues in Kaziranga, miraculously surviving the ravages of the untamed river, but increasingly vulnerable to human intrusion.

KEY SPECIES

MAMMALS One-horned Rhinoceros, Asian Water Buffalo, Tiger, Leopard, Leopard-cat, Fishing Cat, Asian Elephant, Large Indian Civet, Swamp Deer (Barasingha), **Hog-deer** (*above*), Slow Loris, Marbled Cat, Hoolock Gibbon, Capped Langur, Binturong, Yellow-throated Marten, Crab-eating Mongoose, Clawless Otter, Gangetic Dolphin

BIRDS BUSTARDS Bengal Florican **RAPTORS** Pallas's Fish Eagle, Lesser Fish Eagle, Grey-headed Fish Eagle, Osprey, Rufous-bellied Eagle, Pied Harrier, Crested Goshawk, Brown Fish Owl **WOODLAND/SCRUB** Red Junglefowl, Swamp Francolin, Kalij Pheasant, Grey Peacock Pheasant, Great Hornbill, Great Slaty Woodpecker, Dollarbird, Green Imperial Pigeon, Blue-bearded Bee-eater, Chestnut-headed Bee-eater, Red-breasted Parakeet, Long-tailed Broadbill, Maroon Oriole, Golden-crested Myna, Greater Necklaced Laughingthrush, Rufous-necked Laughingthrush, Green Magpie, Collared Treepie, Ruby-cheeked Sunbird **WATERSIDE** Black-necked Stork, Lesser Adjutant, Greater Adjutant, Black Stork, Spot-billed Pelican, Great White Pelican, Fulvous Whistling-duck, Bar-headed Goose, Ruddy Shelduck, White-bellied Heron, Malayan Night Heron, Great Bittern

Additional information on page 131

KEIBUL-LAMJAO NATIONAL PARK

The Brow-antlered Deer or Sangai is a rare species of deer found only in India and Myanmar. It is to be seen in the Keibul-Lamjao National Park of Manipur. An exceptional wilderness area, 32 km from Imphal, the park is situated at Logtak Lake's south-east extremity. Once a famous waterfowl hunting area, this large lake is fringed by deep marshes encrusted with a floating mass of humus, reeds and decaying vegetation, locally known as *phumdi*. Between 30 and 120 cm thick, this mass persists through most of the monsoon season and for a couple of months more. Over the years, cultivation has greatly diminished the extent of these marshes, and Keibul-Lamjao is the largest surviving original habitat of this kind.

According to E P Gee, the celebrated naturalist-photographer, "Keibul Lamjao ... is the only floating wildlife sanctuary in the world." The Sangai has adapted superbly to life in this floating world, and is often seen grazing off the *phumdi* before bounding on to the surrounding harder ground. The *phumdi* has rich organic soil suitable for clusters of grasses and reeds, which often grow several meters tall and are food for the deer. When the water level rises, the Sangai move to the low hills that reach

The peculiar floating vegetation of Keibul-Lamjao is favoured by the rare Brow-antlered Deer.

barely 40-50 m above the *phumdi*.
The top of Pabot Hill and the
observation tower on Chingiao
Hill, the highest point in the park,
offer panoramic views of Keibul-
Lamjao and sometimes of the deer.
The erstwhile princes of
Manipur protected the Sangai deer
as their own hunting interests
extended chiefly to waterfowl.
Later, civil unrest left this animal
vulnerable to persecution. It was
presumed extinct by 1951, but
a couple of years later E P Gee
discovered a few of the Sangai,
whom he dubbed the 'dancing
deer', on Logtak's southern margin.

There are less than 100 Sangai
in the wild, but there are chances
of seeing a few in the course of
a leisurely ride in a dugout canoe.
Other mammals seen here are the
Fishing Cat, the Hog-deer and
the Wild Boar. There have been
reported sightings of Leopard. The
Common Otter, Clawless Otter,
Large and Small Indian Civets
have also been observed. Nearly
100 species of birds, including
waterfowl, herons, rails, crakes and
kingfishers, can be observed here.

All is not well for India's rare
ungulate in this seemingly tranquil
realm. Developmental projects,
social unrest, agriculture, fishing,
livestock grazing and poaching
threaten to annihilate its fragile
world. The Sangai features
prominently in local mythology,
but this alone may not save it for
all time in its only natural home.

KEY SPECIES

**MAMMALS Brow-antlered Deer
(Sangai)** (*above*), Fishing Cat, Leopard,
Hog-deer, Wild Boar, Common Otter,
Large Indian Civet, Small Indian Civet
BIRDS RAPTORS Pallas's Fish Eagle, Grey-
headed Fish Eagle, Pied Harrier, Eurasian
Marsh Harrier, Greater Spotted Eagle,
Peregrine Falcon, Common Kestrel
SCRUB/OPEN AREAS Red Junglefowl,
Manipur Bush Quail, Blue-tailed Bee-eater,
Lesser Coucal, Striated Grassbird, Rufous-
rumped Grassbird, Collared Myna
WATERSIDE Greylag Goose, Fulvous
Whistling-duck, **Bar-headed Goose**
(*below*), Falcated Duck, Ruddy Kingfisher,
Darter, Chinese Pond Heron, Cinnamon
Bittern, Black Bittern, Great Bittern, Great
Crested Grebe, Spot-billed Pelican, Black
Stork, Lesser Adjutant, Greater Adjutant

Additional information on page 131

MANAS TIGER RESERVE

The Manas Tiger Reserve in Assam is a prime spot for viewing wildlife and offers glimpses of the elusive tiger through thick grass cover. At least 20 species of animals found in this park are highly endangered, listed in Schedule I of the International Union of Conservation of Nature Red Data Book. One of these is the famous Golden Langur, discovered only in the mid-20th century. In 1947, C G Baron, a sportsman and naturalist, penned the following lines: "I saw snow white monkeys (langurs)…and so far as I know they are an unidentified species. The whole body and tail is one colour…somewhat like the hair of a blonde." The naturalist E P Gee, authenticated the discovery in 1953 when he recorded the Golden Langur in the forest between the rivers Sankosh and Manas.

Manas is a land of rivers that frequently change their course. The rivers Beki, Hel, Aio, Barnadi, Tanali, Sankosh and Manas gush through the reserve to join the Brahmaputra. This mighty river permeates every aspect of life in Assam, for its people and its wildlife. The reserve, north of the Brahmaputra, spills over into Bhutan where it is known as the Royal Bhutan National Park comprising nearly 1,000 sq km of forested hills.

On the Indian side, a 360 sq km sanctuary was established in 1928 on what was once the hunting preserve of the royal families of Cooch-Behar and Gauripur. In 1973, Project Tiger turned a 2,840 sq km area into a tiger reserve of which almost 500 sq km forms the Manas National Park. Manas's richly variegated landscape and diverse vegetation, from moist-

In Manas, the Asian Water Buffalo can be seen at close quarters from boats and elephant-backs.

deciduous to evergreen, and riverine forests to lush grasslands, and its wide range of endangered species, led it to being declared a World Heritage Site.

Mothanguri, where the river Manas enters India from Bhutan, is a wilderness dominated by the gushing river and forested hills liberally sprinkled with *semul* trees, the pinkish-red flowers blooming in February and March.

Elephant rides, jeep drives and boat trips lead the visitor through remarkable topography and wild and dense vegetation. Of the more than 50 species of mammals here, the Golden Langur, although endangered, is regularly sighted. The 1997 census gives the tiger count as 89. From the riverside, Asian Water Buffalo glare at passing visitors, their horns longer and broader here than elsewhere in India. Gharials (long-snouted crocodiles) bask nearby in the sun. Huge tuskers can also be seen with Gaur, Hog-deer, otters, giant squirrels and various monkeys. The One-horned Rhinoceros is rarely sighted in Manas. Waterside and woodland birds range from tiny resplendent sunbirds to giant hornbills and pelicans.

Unfortunately, unprecedented social unrest and a host of other problems such as expanding tea plantations, poaching and developmental projects continue to threaten one of India's supreme wildlife reserves.

KEY SPECIES

MAMMALS Golden Langur (*above*), Tiger, Leopard, Clouded Leopard, Golden Cat, Leopard-cat, Asian Elephant, Asian Water Buffalo, Gaur (Indian Bison), Swamp Deer (Barasingha), Hog-deer, Pygmy Hog, Capped Langur, Assamese Macaque, Slow Loris, Hispid Hare, Fishing Cat, Marbled Cat, Binturong, Spotted Linsang, Large Indian Civet, Wild Dog (Dhole), Malayan Giant Squirrel, Parti-coloured Flying Squirrel, Crab-eating Mongoose
BIRDS BUSTARDS Bengal Florican
RAPTORS Pallas's Fish Eagle, Lesser Fish Eagle, Osprey, Black Baza, Collared Falconet, Pied Harrier, Rufous-bellied Eagle, Crested Goshawk, Brown Fish Owl
WOODLAND/SCRUB/GRASS Swamp Francolin, Red Junglefowl, Kalij Pheasant, Grey Peacock Pheasant, Great Hornbill, Wreathed Hornbill, Great Slaty Woodpecker, Red-headed Trogon, Long-tailed Broadbill, Dollarbird, Green Imperial Pigeon, Barred Cuckoo-dove, Crow-billed Drongo, Blue-bearded Bee-eater, Coral-billed Scimitar Babbler, Rufous-vented Laughingthrush, Streaked Spiderhunter, Ruby-cheeked Sunbird
WATERSIDE Black Stork, Spot-billed Pelican, Lesser Adjutant, Ruddy Shelduck, Common Merganser, Black-bellied Tern, Black Bittern, Great Cormorant, Crested Kingfisher, Ruddy Kingfisher, Darter

Additional information on page 131

BUXA TIGER RESERVE & JALDAPARA WILDLIFE SANCTUARY

West Bengal forms into a narrow neck that leads from the Ganga deltaic region to the grassy plains (*duars*) and eastern Himalayan foothills, a region teeming with wildlife. The areas of Buxa and Jaldapara are particularly significant as they harbour several endangered species.

The northern boundary of the Buxa Tiger Reserve is fringed by the Sinchula Hills, where the highest altitude is about 1,700 m, and the Sankosh River forms its eastern boundary. Much of the area to the reserve's west and south-west has been altered by tea plantations. The 761 sq km area of Buxa exhibits a range of natural habitats – low, forested foothills, luxuriant *duars*, mixed-deciduous forests, sal, semi-evergreen and evergreen trees, and stretches of moist savannah, cut by rivers from the north that are liable to flood in the rainy season. Massive dolomite mining operations were conducted in this area and it was also marked out as a hunting preserve. Both these activities were carefully monitored in the 1970s and 1980s, and in 1983, over 750 sq km of wilderness was declared a tiger reserve, of which 117 sq km was later demarcated as a national park. Almost 400 species of birds and more than 50 species of mammals, including the Tiger, Asian Elephant, Gaur, Hog-deer, Leopard-cat and Large Indian Civet, prove the value of this habitat.

The One-horned Rhinoceros forms a small population in Jaldapara's splendid forests.

Adjoining the Buxa Tiger Reserve is the 216 sq km Jaldapara Wildlife Sanctuary, an important rhinoceros habitat outside Assam. Nestling in the *duars* and foothills of the eastern Himalaya, the area was given protection as early as the 1940s. It was recognized that the rhinoceros's dwindling population could result from deteriorating habitat. Poaching for rhino horn and expanding human settlements had taken their toll.

Numerous Himalayan rivers, including the wide Torsa, flow through the narrow, low-lying wilderness, which is affected by monsoon floods each year. The Asian Water Buffalo was once seen in the seasonal swamps and pools. Now the rhinoceros finds safe haven there, while the buffalo is confined to Manas and Kaziranga in the east. Floods can be severe, but the wildlife magically survives. Jaldapara is a more rewarding site for viewing animals than Buxa. Small herds of Asian Elephant and Gaur can be encountered here and the most enjoyable way to explore the area is on an elephant-back.

Although Buxa and Jaldapara are both afflicted by natural and human-induced problems, such as flooding, poaching and encroaching agricultural land, plantations and railway lines, it is imperative that these corridors of wildlife that are crucial to the health of the region, be closely monitored and allowed to thrive.

KEY SPECIES

MAMMALS One-horned Rhinoceros, Asian Elephant, Tiger, Leopard, Leopard-cat, Fishing Cat, Marbled Cat, Large Indian Civet, Spotted Linsang, Himalayan Black Bear, Wild Dog (Dhole), Clawless Otter, Assamese Macaque, **Gaur (Indian Bison)** (*above*), Sambar, Spotted Deer (Chital), Hog-deer, Barking Deer, Malayan Giant Squirrel, Parti-coloured Flying Squirrel
BIRDS BUSTARDS Bengal Florican
RAPTORS Pallas's Fish Eagle, Lesser Fish Eagle, Pied Harrier, Crested Goshawk, Oriental Hobby, Grass Owl
WOODLAND/SCRUB/GRASS Swamp Francolin, Black Francolin, Red Junglefowl, Kalij Pheasant, Grey Peacock Pheasant, **Indian Peafowl** (*below*), Great Hornbill, Rufous-necked Hornbill, Great Slaty Woodpecker, Green-billed Malkoha, Red-headed Trogon, Hill Myna, Crow-billed Drongo, Blue-bearded Bee-eater, Green Magpie, White-hooded Babbler, Greater Necklaced Laughingthrush, Rusty-fronted Barwing, Black-throated Sunbird
WATERSIDE Crested Kingfisher

Additional information on page 132

Sunderbans Tiger Reserve

The Sunderbans is a maze of mangrove-encrusted islands amidst a network of tidal creeks and distributaries at the mouth of the Ganga River. The reserve lies to the south-east of Kolkata, West Bengal, and is today a World Heritage Site. This swampy area was partitioned in 1947, and now the larger portion lies with Bangladesh. However, the Indian share of over 4,200 sq km constitutes more than half of the country's mangrove forests. The tiger reserve covers 2,585 sq km of which nearly 1,000 sq km is made up of creeks and waterways.

The best way to move around is to board a motorboat at Canning, Basanti, Gosaba or Sonakhali. A night spent anchored at the edge of a tidal creek, closely watching the dense curtain of mangrove for the elusive, striped cat is an experience beyond compare. According to official estimates, there are nearly 250 tigers, but only if one of the cats chooses to emerge into a clearing is a sighting possible in the thick waterlogged jungle habitat. The Sunderbans tiger is unusual in that it has adapted to the high salinity of the waters and has become almost amphibious, roving between islands or plodding along the edge of a creek at low tide, its coat gleaming with ooze, before vanishing into the tangled forest.

A tangled realm of mangrove forests, Sunderbans is home to a great number of tigers.

The dominant species in the Sunderbans, tigers tend to come into conflict with the intruding human population. Before venturing into the forests, honey-gatherers, woodcutters and fisher-folk pray to the great Tiger God for mercy. Although the conflict at times threatens to undermine all conservation work, the Project Tiger management is taking steps to mitigate the situation. Suggested measures include electrified dummies in fishing boats.

The Jungle Cat, Leopard-cat and Fishing Cat are among the almost 40 mammalian species here, some rather amphibious in their habits. Boat trips can be exciting, providing glimpses of Gangetic Dolphins, Clawless Otters, giant Estuarine Crocodiles and several kinds of turtles including, perhaps, the endangered River Terrapin.

Birds are in plenty with a good range of waterside birds and several woodland species, their numbers augmented in winter by migrants from the north. There are heronries near Sajnekhali, the main tourism zone, and on several other islands. Enduring the varying salinity levels are 400 species of fish, nearly 50 species of reptiles, and a modest floral count of around 120 species.

Ensuring the survival of the complex Sunderbans forest and its wildlife is paramount to our own survival. It is a coastal stabilizer, taming the hostile world of tides and waves to protect the hinterland.

KEY SPECIES

MAMMALS **Tiger** (*above*), Fishing Cat, Leopard-cat, Jungle Cat, Common Palm Civet, Jackal, Gangetic Dolphin, Spotted Deer (Chital), Wild Boar, Clawless Otter, Crab-eating Mongoose, Rhesus Macaque

REPTILES Estuarine Crocodile, Rock Python, King Cobra, **Water Monitor** (*below*), Olive Ridley Turtle, River Terrapin

BIRDS **RAPTORS** Pallas's Fish Eagle, Osprey, Grey-headed Fish Eagle, White-bellied Sea Eagle, Pied Harrier

WOODLAND/SCRUB Red Junglefowl, Blue-tailed Bee-eater, Rufous Treepie, Greater Coucal, Blue-throated Barbet

WATERSIDE Masked Finfoot, Asian Openbill, Lesser Adjutant, Greater Adjutant, Oriental Stork, Brown-winged Kingfisher, Stork-billed Kingfisher, Collared Kingfisher, Ruddy Kingfisher

Additional information on page 133

SIMLIPAL TIGER RESERVE

The Simlipal Tiger Reserve, one of the country's largest protected areas, is located in the Mayurbhanj district of Orissa. A forested, hilly terrain 200 km south-west of Kolkata, the reserve is endowed with an exceptional biodiversity. Its name derives from the abundance of *semul* or red silk cotton trees which bloom vividly in the first few months of the year. Of the reserve's almost 1,000 species of flowering plants, 94 are orchids alone, many of which are on show at the small orchidarium at Gurguria.

Simlipal's hilly terrain is carved by a number of rivulets. The riparian habitat around streams such as East Deo, Palpala, Budhabalang, Khadkei, Khairi and Bandhan contains swampy tracts and impressive waterfalls, the finest and most popular being Barheipani and Joranda. Expanses of semi-evergreen and moist-deciduous forests are interspersed with majestic sal trees and lowland meadows. Grassy Chahala, Bachurichara, Devsthali and Sapaghar have fairly good concentrations of wildlife.

Three of India's bigger animal species – Tiger, Asian Elephant and Gaur – are resident here, but the terrain and vegetation make sightings rare.

Between December and March, the rutting Chital stags often spar for control over their herd.

From the leafy canopy, the giant squirrel's rattling cry merges with the din of the nearly 250 species of birds. Crocodiles and otters can be seen along the rivers. A captive-breeding project, the Mugger Crocodile Scheme at Jashipur, towards the north-west fringes of the reserve, aims to restore to Simlipal a viable population of the Mugger (Marsh Crocodile).

The reserve was the hunting preserve of the Mayurbhanj maharajas. A small area was declared a sanctuary in 1957. The tiger reserve extends over 2,750 sq km, within a larger area of 4,374 sq km that constitutes the biosphere reserve. An 845 sq km core area comprises the Simlipal National Park, a tract of total wilderness. The forest department organizes jungle visits, but accommodation has been kept to the minimum in the reserve's much-visited northern part. Unfortunately, certain areas have degenerated into picnic spots.

Excessive hunting in the past seriously damaged the wildlife of Simlipal. Local tribal communities still indulge in an annual ritual hunt (akhand shikar) with bows and arrows. Encroachment, livestock grazing, poaching and indifferent visitors add to the problems. Despite nature's resilience, better funding for effective protection and awareness is crucial to the maintenance of this wilderness, which may still be able to sustain healthy numbers of animals.

KEY SPECIES

MAMMALS Tiger, Leopard, Leopard-cat, Jungle Cat, Wild Dog (Dhole), Wolf, Striped Hyena, Small Indian Civet, Ratel, Sloth Bear, Asian Elephant, Gaur (Indian Bison), Sambar, Spotted Deer (Chital), Barking Deer, Mouse Deer, Chowsingha (Four-horned Antelope), Indian Pangolin
REPTILES Mugger (Marsh Crocodile), King Cobra, Rock Python
BIRDS RAPTORS Crested Serpent Eagle, Black Eagle, Oriental Honey-buzzard, **Changeable Hawk Eagle** (above), Booted Eagle, Peregrine Falcon, Dusky Eagle Owl, Brown Hawk Owl
WOODLAND/SCRUB/GRASS Painted Spurfowl, Red Spurfowl, Red Junglefowl, Grey Francolin, Malabar Pied Hornbill, Lineated Barbet, Malabar Trogon, Blue-bearded Bee-eater, Chestnut-headed Bee-eater, Blue-faced Malkoha, Asian Fairy Bluebird, Spangled Drongo, Black-naped Oriole, Hill Myna, Large Woodshrike, Scaly Thrush, White-rumped Shama, Striped Tit Babbler, Crimson Sunbird
WATERSIDE Stork-billed Kingfisher

Additional information on page 134

BHITARKANIKA WILDLIFE SANCTUARY & GAHIRMATHA MARINE WILDLIFE SANCTUARY

Bhitarkanika, India's second-largest mangrove, is on the cyclone-prone coast of Orissa. Here also lies Gahirmatha, the site of the world's largest congregation of sea-turtles. Both these areas are in the deltaic region of the rivers Brahmani, Baitarani and Dhamra, which originate in the Chota Nagpur Plateau. As they approach the Bay of Bengal, they transform into slow, winding waterways, depositing nutrient-rich silt along a network of creeks and inlets. This region is a mix of mangroves, tropical forests, creeks, mudflats, grasslands, scrublands, sandy beaches and offshore islands.

Gahirmatha is a beach on Bhitarkanika's eastern boundary and it stretches for nearly 30 km. It is renowned for the Olive Ridley Turtle of which more than half a million congregate here between December and April every year. Instinct draws the turtles from the sea, dragging their ponderous forms onto the coast where they dig into the sand to lay their eggs, before skilfully covering them up and returning to the boundless sea with the incoming tide. This seasonal event, known as *arribada* (arrival) in Spanish, occurs at four main sites, two in Costa Rica, one in Mexico, and the largest, discovered in 1974, at Gahirmatha. Dr H R Bustard, a Food

Gahirmatha's sandy stretch of coast attracts one of the largest congregations of nesting sea-turtles.

and Agricultural Organisation (FAO) consultant, urged the Indian government to protect this unique nesting-ground. In 1975, a 672 sq km area of Bhitarkanika was declared a sanctuary, and a 145 sq km core upgraded to national park in 1988. Then, in 1997, a large section of the sea off Gahirmatha and the fringing coastal lands were named as a separate sanctuary, but contiguous with Bhitarkanika.

Apart from road-links from Cuttack and Bhadrak to Rajnagar and Chandbali in Bhitarkanika, the region is traversable only by boat. Habalikhati, Ekakula, Dangmal and Gupti are areas representative of the region's unusual wildlife. This land, with a humid, tropical climate and ample rainfall, has a rich biodiversity. The mangroves support a varied and crowded marine world. A vast range of fish species is to be found in the waters together with India's largest reptile, the endangered Estuarine Crocodile. Water Monitor, numerous snakes, and mammals such as Spotted Deer, Wild Boar, Sambar and Fishing Cat are also found here. There are nearly 200 bird species, and the Bagagahana heronry near Suajore Creek throngs with waterbirds. There is an impressive range of wintering waterfowl, waders (sandpipers, plovers, godwits and curlews), gulls and terns.

Unfortunately, Olive Ridley Turtles, the main attraction, suffer a high mortality rate. Mechanized boats are the chief culprits, and perhaps small-scale fishing operations unwittingly cause fatalities. Operation Kachhapa has been launched for the turtles' protection, a non-mechanized fishing zone has been established, nesting sites monitored and efforts made to improve awareness amongst the local people.

KEY SPECIES

MAMMALS Fishing Cat, Jungle Cat, Leopard-cat, Gangetic Dolphin, Striped Hyena, Smooth Indian Otter, Small Indian Civet, Spotted Deer (Chital), Sambar, Jackal, Indian Porcupine
REPTILES Leatherback Sea Turtle, Olive Ridley Turtle, Green Sea Turtle, Hawksbill Sea Turtle, Estuarine Crocodile, Water Monitor, **King Cobra** (*above*)
BIRDS RAPTORS White-bellied Sea Eagle, Peregrine Falcon, Osprey, Short-toed Eagle, Eurasian Marsh Harrier, Pied Harrier, Steppe Eagle, Greater Spotted Eagle
WATERSIDE Great Cormorant, Darter, Great Egret, Grey Heron, Cinnamon Bittern, Black Ibis, Spot-billed Pelican, Painted Stork, Asian Openbill, Lesser Adjutant, Stork-billed Kingfisher, Black-capped Kingfisher, Collared Kingfisher, Pied Kingfisher

Additional information on page 134

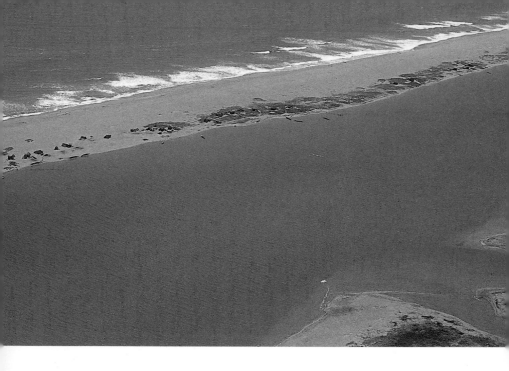

Nalaban (Chilka) Wildlife Sanctuary

The Chilka Lake is a vast lagoon of more than 1,000 sq km of shallow waters, shielded from the Bay of Bengal by a long and narrow sandy bar. Islands lie scattered in the lagoon, the most prominent being Kalijai, Nalaban, Parikud and Mahisavarahampura. The Chilka lagoon receives fresh water and sediment from many rivers, particularly the Daya, the Bhargavi, the Nuna, the Kusumi and the Salia. The Nalaban Wildlife Sanctuary, declared a site of international importance in the 1970s, is situated on one of the larger islands.

   Between 4 km and 30 km wide, the Chilka Lake sprawls from 30 km south-west of Puri in Orissa for nearly 70 km. The long sandy bar has just a narrow opening to the sea, but the lagoon's ecology is an interplay between sea water and fresh water. Salinity levels vary and are lowest in the monsoon months. The lagoon's narrow opening to the sea is believed to be becoming steadily smaller and is leading to the lagoon's decline. The freshwater content is increasing and silt accumulating from numerous streams in Chilka's northern fringe has given rise to large areas of freshwater weeds. Ironically, the same natural forces that created the lagoon are now playing a vital role in changing its face.

A narrow sand-bar all but separates Chilka from sea, bestowing it with a distinctive environment.

A break in the rocky, coastal lineaments in south Orissa some 5,000 years ago is said to have brought about the existence of Chilka Lake. Massive marine inundation first created an open bay on which a maritime trade post was established. Over the years, sand-laden littoral currents steadily and relentlessly built a ridge enclosing an enormous lagoon between the sea on the one side and hills and rivers on the other.

The lagoon is one of India's great avian spectacles. The main attraction at the 15 sq km island of Nalaban is the congregation of waterbirds, both waterfowl (ducks, geese) and waders (sandpipers, plovers, herons, storks, flamingos), besides thousands of gulls and terns, which throng here during winter, joined by legions of raptors.

The sparse grass and scrub and foreshore areas of the sandy bar host small numbers of Blackbuck, Spotted Deer, Jackal and Jungle Cat, besides hyenas and hares. Dolphins are sometimes sighted, both in the sea and in the lagoon waters. Chilka Lake shelters about 150 species of fish on which almost 25,000 fisherfolk are dependent for their livelihood. The area is beset today by rising corporate demands for large-scale prawn- and fish-farming and tourism. If well-managed, tourism could help in preserving the wilderness.

Chilka offers several sites of interest along its inland edge, easily accessible by both road and train. Rambha, Barkul and Balugaon lie on the west side of the lake en route to Bhubhaneshwar from Gopalpur-on-Sea, while Satapada, on the seaward side, is 48 km from Puri. Motorboat and kayak rides offer insights into rural lifestyles and Chilka's wildlife.

KEY SPECIES

MAMMALS Blackbuck, Spotted Deer (Chital), Jackal, Striped Hyena, Jungle Cat, Black-naped Hare, Common Mongoose, Indian Porcupine, Gangetic Dolphin
BIRDS RAPTORS White-bellied Sea Eagle, **Pallas's Fish Eagle** (*above*), Osprey, Short-toed Eagle, Eurasian Marsh Harrier, Steppe Eagle, Peregrine Falcon
SCRUB/OPEN AREAS Grey Francolin, Blue-tailed Bee-eater, Oriental Pratincole
WATERSIDE Greater Flamingo, Lesser Flamingo, Great White Pelican, Spot-billed Pelican, Painted Stork, Greylag Goose, Bar-headed Goose, Ruddy Shelduck, Red-crested Pochard, Eurasian Spoonbill, Pied Avocet, Eurasian Curlew, Black-tailed Godwit, Broad-billed Sandpiper, Asian Dowitcher, Black-capped Kingfisher, Caspian Tern, Great Crested Tern, Pallas's Gull, Collared Kingfisher

Additional information on page 135

SOUTHERN ZONE

*At the heart of the southern peninsula is
a tangled tropical realm fringed by fertile
coastal tracts and an arid inland region.
The Nilgiri, Annamalai, Palni, Cardamom,
Nallamalai and Ashambu hills, together with
the Western Ghats, present an array of
habitats from pristine forest and grassy hill-
slopes, drained by gushing streams, to placid
rivers and gigantic, artificial reservoirs. Home
of the majestic Asian Elephant, the zone
also provides a haven for some of India's
most threatened but little known life-forms.*

NAGARJUNASAGAR-SRISAILAM TIGER RESERVE

Nagarjunasagar dam on the Krishna River in Andhra Pradesh is one of the world's largest masonry dams. It is named after Acharya Nagarjuna, an eminent Buddhist scholar who, in approximately AD 150, founded a centre of learning in this area. Forgotten over time, evidence of the centre was unearthed in the early 1900s. In 1950, when the site was chosen for an irrigation-cum-hydropower reservoir, the excavated sculptures and rare artefacts were reconstructed on Nagarjunaconda Island in the middle of the vast, flooding reservoir, a 45-minute boat ride from the dam. Other interesting archaeological sites remain on the banks of the Krishna River that flows for nearly 125 km through the Nagarjunasagar-Srisailam Tiger Reserve, dividing it into northern and southern sections. This is India's largest tiger reserve and includes in its area the Srisailam dam, which is also on the Krishna River.

The reserve, 3,568 sq km in area, extends over the several plateaus of the Nallamalai Hills, the most prominent being the Amrabad Plateau in the northern section. A variety of forest types can be seen in the dramatic gorges and valleys carved by the Krishna, from thorn-scrub to dry- and mixed-deciduous and sheltered patches of semi-evergreen. There is an abundance of bamboo in this rugged wilderness.

The great congregations of wildlife, as witnessed in some of India's reserves, are missing here, although there is a wide range of species.

The backlit antlers of a Chital lend a marvellous mood to the forests of India's largest tiger reserve.

Tigers are reclusive and chances of sighting them are rare. Animals typical of deciduous Indian forests, such as Leopard, Wolf and Sloth Bear, are mostly present, but there are no Gaur or Asian Elephant.

Bird-watching is the most rewarding activity here with some 200 species on view, including wintering waterfowl on the reservoirs. Nature walks, jeep drives and boat rides on the river can keep the visitor well occupied. A morning spent in a circular bamboo-and-hide coracle makes a pleasant change. The Chandravanka stream cascades down for over 15 m at the Ethiopothala Falls, 12 km downstream from Nagarjunasagar dam. A crocodile-breeding centre has been established nearby and an environment educational centre is operational at Srisailam.

Signs of human intrusion are quite apparent in certain areas of the reserve. The Chenchus, a tribal community, live here in their quaint bamboo homes called *gudems*. Visits to their settlements can be arranged. The temple at Srisailam within the protected area attracts many pilgrims. This region is part of a Naxalite stronghold, causing some social unrest and leading to problems in the reserve's management. The wilderness requires considerable attention, however, despite the dearth of major animal populations, as it plays a significant role in the Eastern Ghats' ecosystem.

KEY SPECIES

MAMMALS Tiger, Leopard, Sloth Bear, Wild Dog (Dhole), Striped Hyena, Wolf, Small Indian Civet, Ratel, Sambar, Spotted Deer (Chital), Barking Deer, Nilgai (Blue Bull), Indian Pangolin, Indian Giant Squirrel, Common Langur

BIRDS RAPTORS Bonelli's Eagle, Changeable Hawk Eagle, Crested Serpent Eagle, Oriental Honey-buzzard, White-eyed Buzzard, Osprey, Short-toed Snake Eagle, Common Kestrel

WOODLAND/SCRUB Grey Junglefowl, Indian Peafowl, Grey Francolin, Painted Spurfowl, Red Spurfowl, Indian Grey Hornbill, Rufous Woodpecker, Lesser Yellownape, Emerald Dove, Yellow-footed Green Pigeon, Painted Sandgrouse, Indian Cuckoo, Blue-faced Malkoha, **Sirkeer Malkoha** (*above*), Alpine Swift, Black-hooded Oriole, Black-headed Cuckooshrike, Large Cuckooshrike, Spangled Drongo

WATERSIDE Large Cormorant, Eurasian Thick-knee, Yellow-wattled Lapwing, Grey Heron, Black Ibis, Stork-billed Kingfisher

Additional information on page 136

Ranganathittu Wildlife Sanctuary

A weir was built across the Kaveri River in the mid-17th century, 16 km north of Mysore in present-day Karnataka, to divert water to the island-fort of Srirangapatnam. This fort is famous as the bastion of Hyder Ali and Tipu Sultan, powerful rulers of a large chunk of southern India in the 18th century, who for a long while successfully stalled British colonial interests in the country. A couple of kilometres upstream from Srirangapatnam is Ranganathittu, one of the many small islands that emerged when the weir was built. When Salim Ali, the renowned ornithologist, conducted a survey of the Mysore region, he found these relatively newly-developed islands had attracted large avian populations. Mugger (Marsh Crocodile) and other wildlife were also present. A sanctuary was declared in 1940 comprising many of the islands and named after the 0.67 sq km Ranganathittu, the island with the main concentration of nesting birds. However, many birds feed and rest on the neighbouring islands as well.

Ranganathittu's small area belies its wealth of life-forms. It is an unusual sanctuary, a tiny island in the Kaveri, isolated and overgrown with vegetation. Large trees are the refuge of waterbirds. Egrets, herons, ibises, cormorants, pelicans, openbills and spoonbills breed between May and early September. The breeding season comes to these southern riverine islands early in the year when compared to north and central India,

Giant Muggers can often be seen basking on the rocks in the Kaveri River, offering close encounters.

undoubtedly encouraged by the
high organic content of the
surrounding agricultural tracts and
the seasonal flow-levels of the river.
Apart from a few raptors, the
nesting birds are also safer from
people and most predators.

River Terns and Great Thick-
knees breed on the rocks in the
summer months, but it is the
nesting waterbirds that transform
Ranganathittu into a flurry of
featherfolk, hauling twigs,
constructing nests, skirmishing over
sites, mating and feeding raucous,
hungry fledglings. Between late July
and October, the sanctuary is
crowded with young birds perched
on low branches or on the jutting
rocks. Basking on these rocks are
also some enormous crocodiles.
Other species include Smooth
Indian Otter, Bonnet Macaque and
huge congregations of bats,
especially the Indian Flying Fox,
countless numbers of which are
seen roosting on larger trees.

Ranganathittu is no less exciting
after the residents have reared their
young. Now arrive the winter
migrants – ducks, waders, wagtails,
swallows and birds of prey. The
south bank of the river offers
excellent opportunities for sighting
birds. The forest department
organizes boat and coracle rides
facilitating close encounters with
the wildlife, but it is imperative to
maintain a reasonable distance
during the breeding season out of
consideration for the nesting birds.

KEY SPECIES

MAMMALS Jackal, Smooth Indian Otter,
Bonnet Macaque, Black-naped Hare, Wild
Boar, Flying Fox
REPTILES Mugger (Marsh Crocodile)
BIRDS RAPTORS Osprey, Grey-headed
Fish Eagle, Eurasian Marsh Harrier, Black-
shouldered Kite, Brahminy Kite, Pallid
Harrier, Shikra
WOODLAND/SCRUB Black-rumped
Flameback, Rufous Treepie, Eurasian
Golden Oriole, Asian Paradise-flycatcher
WATERSIDE Great Cormorant, Darter,
Great Egret, **Intermediate Egret** (*below*),
Purple Heron, Asian Openbill, Eurasian
Spoonbill, Black-headed Ibis, Spot-billed
Pelican, Painted Stork, Spotbill Duck,
Lesser Whistling-duck, **River Tern** (*above*),
Black-bellied Tern, Black-winged Stilt,
Great Thick-knee, Wire-tailed Swallow,
Pied Kingfisher, White-browed Wagtail

Additional information on page 136

NAGARHOLE NATIONAL PARK

Nagarhole, among India's most well-managed wildlife reserves, is situated in the vast wilds between the Western Ghats and the Nilgiris. Endowed with numerous winding streams, the Nagarhole National Park lies in the picturesque Coorg region of southern Karnataka. The better-known rivers are the Nagarhole or Cobra, the Kabini, the Taraka, the Lakshmanateertha and the Sarathi. The Nagarhole area falls just north-west of Bandipur, but it is comparatively less hilly. Masalbetta at 957 m is its highest point.

This region, especially the forests of Kakkankote in its south, was the private hunting ground of the prosperous princely state of Mysore. The tall, luxuriant forests are a mix of moist-deciduous and tropical semi-evergreen, interspersed with scrub and grassy swamplands, known locally as *hadlus*, and a favourite site of herbivores, especially elephant and gaur. There are also large numbers of deer. Nagarhole is the first site in India to achieve success with radio-collaring of tigers, an important tool for ecological studies.

The stately teak forests, relatively undisturbed in some areas, include India's older teak plantations, dating to the mid-1800s. A 285 sq km tract was declared a wildlife sanctuary in 1955, and in 1988 a larger area was upgraded to a national park. Some of the landscape was altered in 1974 when an irrigation dam on the Kabini River created a vast reservoir that

On the extensive banks of the Kabini Reservoir, large herds of the Asian Elephant can be seen.

now forms the boundary between Bandipur and Nagarhole.

On the banks of the reservoir, at Mastigudi, are the remains of an elephant-capturing operation established by Hyder Ali, the 18th-century ruler of Mysore. He was reportedly unsuccessful, but later, the same *khedda* or the stockade technique of trapping elephants was used with good result. In a little less than a century from 1873, more than 1,500 wild elephants were captured and several hundred killed or injured. The last *khedda* was held as recently as the early 1970s.

The breathtaking, panoramic sweep of the backwaters is dotted with wild elephants, sometimes a couple of hundred of them, accompanied by Gaur, Sambar, Spotted Deer and otters, and perhaps a few crocodiles at the water's edge. Myriad forest birds, including hornbills, woodpeckers and drongos call in flawless symphony. Karapura, Mastigudi and Nagarhole divisions of the park are favoured for wildlife viewing and remain treasured memories.

Riding in a jeep or open van is the best way to experience Nagarhole's wilds, but a coracle ride leaves a lingering impression. Drifting lazily down the waters in the circular bamboo boat, the visitor can get very close views of the cormorants and darters perched on the submerged tree-trunks of the reservoir, and at times also of the lordly elephant.

KEY SPECIES

MAMMALS Asian Elephant, Gaur (Indian Bison), Tiger, Leopard, Wild Dog (Dhole), Leopard-cat, Rusty Spotted Cat, Small Indian Civet, Striped-necked Mongoose, Ruddy Mongoose, Sloth Bear, Indian Giant Squirrel, Sambar, Spotted Deer (Chital), Barking Deer, Mouse Deer, Chowsingha (Four-horned Antelope), Indian Pangolin

BIRDS **RAPTORS** Changeable Hawk Eagle, Besra, Crested Goshawk, Crested Serpent Eagle, Jerdon's Baza, Osprey, Brown Fish Owl, Mottled Wood Owl

WOODLAND/SCRUB Grey Junglefowl, **Indian Peafowl** (*above*), Red Spurfowl, Painted Spurfowl, Painted Bush Quail, Great Hornbill, Malabar Pied Hornbill, White-bellied Woodpecker, Greater Flameback, Malabar Parakeet, Green Imperial Pigeon, Malabar Trogon, Chestnut-headed Bee-eater, Spangled Drongo, Greater Racket-tailed Drongo, Asian Fairy Bluebird, Hill Myna, Crimson-backed Sunbird

WATERSIDE Great Cormorant, Asian Openbill, Painted Stork, Lesser Whistling-duck, Stork-billed Kingfisher

Additional information on page 137

BANDIPUR TIGER RESERVE

Occasionally, a herd of wild elephants blocks the busy highway from Bangalore to Udhagamandalam (Ooty). This road passes through the expansive, relatively intact 5,520 sq km area of the Nilgiri Biosphere Reserve, a viable elephant habitat that includes Bandipur and the adjoining Mudumalai, Nagarhole and Wynaad wildlife reserves.

The Bandipur forests of Karnataka have been officially protected for over a hundred years and no timber felling or hunting was allowed. As long ago as 1898, a small area was declared a sanctuary, and by 1941 the Venugopal Wildlife Park was established on nearly 800 sq km, the small inner core being Bandipur. Project Tiger, launched in 1973, recognized the importance of this tract for elephant, tiger and other wildlife, and Bandipur Tiger Reserve was born on an 874 sq km area, which included most of the Venugopal Park.

Gopalaswamy Betta, the highest point in the reserve, has a panoramic view of gently sloping mountains, flat-topped hills and gorges encrusted with largely mixed-deciduous forest. Bamboo stands are interspersed with grassy carpets, giving a park-like quality to some of the terrain. Bandipur's beauty can be attributed to the two monsoons, the south-west and the

In the shadow of the Western Ghats, Bandipur is part of south India's largest contiguous wilderness.

north-east, that bring in rainfall well through the year, and to the fact that it is almost at the juncture of the Deccan Plateau and the outer spurs of the Western Ghats.

These open woodlands offer excellent opportunities for viewing wildlife. The Kabini River, a tributary of the Kaveri, runs along the park's north-west precincts. Beyond the backwaters of the Kabini Reservoir lies the Nagarhole National Park. Wild elephants can be seen along this stretch of river. The rivers Mulahole, Nugu and Moyar meander through Bandipur and, from a point known as Rolling Rocks, there is an excellent view of the Moyar River's impressive gorge.

Bandipur Tiger Reserve falls midway between Ooty and the city of Mysore and is easily accessible. The 82 sq km tourism zone allows most of the area in the reserve to remain undisturbed. Roads skirt numerous salt-licks and water pools frequented by a wide range of animals such as Tiger, Leopard, Wild Dog and Sloth Bear. There is plenty of bird activity. Herds of elephant are common as are the majestic gaur. These great oxen, wrongly known as the Indian Bison, staged a remarkable comeback after the disastrous rinderpest epidemic of the late 1960s. Large herds of Spotted Deer can be seen around the Bandipur tourism zone every evening. The profusion and accessibility of its wildlife makes Bandipur a popular destination.

KEY SPECIES

MAMMALS Asian Elephant, Gaur (Indian Bison), **Tiger** (*above*), Leopard, Wild Dog (Dhole), Sloth Bear, Leopard-cat, Small Indian Civet, Common Palm Civet, Striped-necked Mongoose, Ruddy Mongoose, Sambar, Spotted Deer (Chital), Barking Deer, Mouse Deer, Indian Pangolin, Indian Giant Squirrel

BIRDS RAPTORS Changeable Hawk Eagle, Bonelli's Eagle, Crested Serpent Eagle, Besra, Crested Goshawk, Mottled Wood Owl, Brown Hawk Owl

WOODLAND/SCRUB Grey Junglefowl, Red Spurfowl, Grey Francolin, Painted Spurfowl, Malabar Pied Hornbill, White-bellied Woodpecker, Malabar Trogon, Chestnut-headed Bee-eater, Blue-bearded Bee-eater, Vernal Hanging Parrot, Blue-faced Malkoha, Velvet-fronted Nuthatch, Black-headed Cuckooshrike, Hill Myna, White-bellied Drongo, Greater Racket-tailed Drongo, Green Imperial Pigeon, Asian Paradise-flycatcher, Bar-winged Flycatcher-shrike, Scarlet Minivet

Additional information on page 137

MUDUMALAI WILDLIFE SANCTUARY

Mudumalai, in the extreme west of Tamil Nadu, is an ecologically rich terrain, despite being in the rain-shadow of the Nilgiris. With Bandipur in the north, the region forms a single, continuous viable habitat for a varied range of wildlife. While Mudumalai's western half experiences the south-west monsoon, the eastern tracts feel the relatively gentler north-east monsoon a little later, and this results in a diversity of vegetation types.

Tropical moist-deciduous vegetation towards the western parts of the sanctuary gives way to dry-deciduous and thorn-scrub along the east, supporting a few blackbucks. An erstwhile game reserve, Mudumalai was declared a wildlife sanctuary with a 62 sq km area in the early 1940s. Today, the sanctuary and the national park together extend over an area of 321 sq km, and are a mix of low hills, valleys and flat terrain sprinkled with a few swampy areas. There is considerable movement of animals in this vital wildlife corridor area, and the clear days from late January to early April are most rewarding for the wildlife enthusiast.

Tigers are largely elusive but leopards are more visible. However, the most feared hunter of this area is the Wild Dog, and a pack on the move is not an uncommon sight. Mudumalai's main attraction is the large herds of

Mudumalai is one of the reserves that form the last wild frontier of the region's fascinating wildlife.

herbivores such as deer, gaur and elephant. The gaur recovered from a rinderpest epidemic in the late 1960s, and now some of the finest specimens are seen here, their bulky frames in tune with this perfect habitat. Elephant herds and solitary males, including tuskless male elephants or *makhanas*, are a regular sight. The renowned big game hunting sites of yore – Umbetta, Masinagudi, Kargudi – still host a variety of Indian wildlife.

Mudumalai is reasonably well organized. The well-planned paths are best traversed by jeep or open vans, while elephant-back is advised for areas with tall grass and along stream-beds. Several trails skirt waterholes where plenty of animal activity can be seen. The scream of the Indian Giant Squirrel can be heard from the leafy canopy high above, and a mélange of woodland birds adds to the thrill of the forest. The summit of Kargudi Hill offers a strikingly panoramic view of the sanctuary and the Moyar Gorge.

More elephants have been born at Theppakadu, the elephant camp near Mudumalai's reception centre, than elsewhere in India. The camp offers an interesting glimpse into the life of captive elephants. Despite a wealth of species, this sanctuary is struggling to survive against the demands of human settlements, cattle grazing, forest fires, developmental projects and a busy highway. Protecting this area remains a challenging task.

KEY SPECIES

MAMMALS Asian Elephant (*above*), Gaur (Indian Bison), Tiger, Leopard, Wild Dog (Dhole), Striped Hyena, Leopard-cat, Rusty Spotted Cat, Small Indian Civet, Striped-necked Mongoose, Ruddy Mongoose, Sloth Bear, Indian Giant Squirrel, Sambar, Spotted Deer (Chital), Barking Deer, Mouse Deer, Chowsingha (Four-horned Antelope), Indian Pangolin

BIRDS RAPTORS Changeable Hawk Eagle, Black Eagle, Oriental Honey-buzzard, Jerdon's Baza, Bonelli's Eagle, Crested Goshawk, Besra, Mottled Wood Owl, Brown Hawk Owl

WOODLAND/SCRUB Grey Junglefowl, Red Spurfowl, Grey Francolin, Painted Spurfowl, Painted Bush Quail, White-bellied Woodpecker, Lesser Yellownape, Greater Flameback, Streak-throated Woodpecker, Chestnut-headed Bee-eater, Emerald Dove, Green Imperial Pigeon, Pompadour Green Pigeon, Grey-bellied Cuckoo, Indian Cuckoo, Alpine Swift, Black-hooded Oriole, Greater Racket-tailed Drongo, Black-headed Cuckooshrike, Grey-headed Bulbul, Forest Wagtail, Crimson-backed Sunbird, Loten's Sunbird

Additional information on page 138

SILENT VALLEY NATIONAL PARK

The Silent Valley National Park in Kerala state is nearly 150 km from
the noisy, industrial city of Coimbatore. Its recorded history goes back
no further than 150 years, but this wilderness received unprecedented
attention in the late 1970s and early 1980s as a possible site for a
hydroelectric project. Local, national and international conservation
organizations combined successfully against the project and, instead,
a 90 sq km area was declared a national park in 1984.

   Known locally as Sairandhrivanam, the Silent Valley is one of the few
tracts of virgin tropical evergreen forest that are still to be seen in India.
One of the reasons the valley is referred to as 'silent' is the near absence
of cicadas, insects that can make even normal conversation difficult when
they set up a clamour. Despite a wealth of other highly vocal creatures,
all that can be heard in this park is the hushed murmur of a few visitors.
A lack of easy access, difficult terrain and strict protection has kept these
forests more or less intact, apart from some selective logging in the early
1900s. It is a scantily inhabited area, the closest neighbours being the
tribal Mudakars of the Attappady Valley.

The perennial Kuntipuzha River flows through the Silent Valley, sustaining a thriving ecosystem.

Silent Valley is in the Kundali Hills of the Western Ghats, a tableland enclosed by high ridges and steep escarpments, ascending in the east to the Upper Nilgiri Plateau. Altitude ranges from 650 m to over 2,000 m, and flowing through the park is the shallow, perennial Kuntipuzha River that splits Silent Valley into a broad eastern segment and a narrower western one. Smaller rivers originate in the park's high, eastern frontiers to merge with the Kuntipuzha. The gushing waters and lush forests are a genetic storehouse of indescribable variety. A wide range of fish species are said to swim these waters. The Kerala Forest Research Institute is conducting various ecological studies in this area, with a special focus on the local flora and the Lion-tailed Macaque.

The medley of habitat types – dense tropical evergreen, sub-tropical hill forest, evergreen sholas and grasslands to Kuntipuzha's west and on the high eastern slopes – support innumerable species.

There are almost 1,000 species of flowering plants, such as the *Aeginetia* (*right*), about 40 species of mammals, nearly 150 of birds, 19 of amphibians, and countless insects and small creatures. Several rare bat species are said to occur here. Elephants, tigers, macaques, flying squirrels, hornbills, sunbirds and birdwings can be seen in this region of intense natural beauty.

KEY SPECIES

MAMMALS Asian Elephant, Nilgiri Tahr, Tiger, Wild Dog (Dhole), Nilgiri Marten, Rusty Spotted Cat, Small Indian Civet, Striped-necked Mongoose, Brown Mongoose, Lion-tailed Macaque, Slender Loris, Large Brown Flying Squirrel, Grizzled Giant Squirrel, Mouse Deer
REPTILES Malabar Pit Viper (*above*)
BIRDS RAPTORS Black Eagle, Crested Goshawk, Rufous-bellied Eagle, Jerdon's Baza, Mountain Hawk Eagle, Crested Serpent Eagle, Besra, Brown Wood Owl
WOODLAND/SCRUB Grey Junglefowl, Painted Bush Quail, Red Spurfowl, Sri Lanka Frogmouth, Great-eared Nightjar, Great Hornbill, Malabar Pied Hornbill, Malabar Grey Hornbill, White-bellied Woodpecker, Dollarbird, Malabar Trogon, Asian Fairy Bluebird, Blue-bearded Bee-eater, Grey-breasted Laughingthrush, Hill Myna, Mountain Imperial Pigeon, Nilgiri Wood Pigeon, Black-and-orange Flycatcher, Nilgiri Flycatcher, Malabar Whistling Thrush, Wynaad Laughingthrush, Little Spiderhunter

Additional information on page 139

INDIRA GANDHI (ANNAMALAI) NATIONAL PARK & PARAMBIKULAM WILDLIFE SANCTUARY

The Annamalais or 'Mountains of the Elephant' lie in the High Ranges, within the Western Ghats, yet they are geologically distinct. Much of this landscape has been altered by tea, coffee and spice plantations, but a few wildlife sites still remain. The inaccessibility of the Annamalais ensured that it was left largely untouched. The Kongunadu country around Annamalai was a part of the medieval Vijayanagar empire. Under British control, vast areas of forest were cleared on the high plateaus for teak, tea, coffee and cardamom plantations. With them went much of the wildlife.

The foothills are less than 300 m in altitude, but the Annamalais then rise to a series of plateaus. The Topslip-Parambikulam Plateau (800 m) ascends to the Valparai Plateau, between 1,000 and 1,250 m, in the heart of the plantations. The elevation range ensures an array of habitats. Dry thorn forests in the low foothills lead to mixed-deciduous and tropical semi-evergreen stretches. Above the Valparai Plateau are grass-hills and *sholas*, or dense evergreen forests. In this montane world several species of plants and animals have their closest kin only in the distant Himalaya.

The Indira Gandhi Wildlife Sanctuary and National Park extends over this region for approximately 960 sq km. Although this reserve lies in Tamil

Annamalai is a mix of dense deciduous forests and evergreen sholas *amid spectacular mountains.*

Nadu, it is contiguous with Kerala's
Parambikulam Wildlife Sanctuary in
the west and Eravikulam National
Park in the south. Inhabiting this
verdant realm of dense forest and
grassland are many endangered
species such as the Nilgiri Langur,
the Lion-tailed Macaque and the
Nilgiri Tahr, the last a type of wild
goat. The continuous wilderness
area, which is created by the
other adjoining sanctuaries, is an
important biodiversity hotspot with
an incredible wealth of life.

Despite their physical proximity,
Annamalai and Parambikulam are
very different. Annamalai is hilly
and undulating with montane forest
and grass-hills, while Parambikulam
is a web of thick deciduous and
semi-evergreen forest, picturesquely
set around artificial reservoirs.
Much of the wildlife is, however,
similar, the dominant species being
the Gaur. There are also a fair
number of elephants.

The Annamalai-Parambikulam
forests are of unparalleled beauty.
The largest teak and rosewood trees
are known to occur in these forests.
Writing in *Records of Sport in
Southern India* (1952), General
Douglas Hamilton said, "The views
from this mountain are the grandest
and most extensive I have ever
beheld...." Over half a century
earlier, W T Hornaday wrote in
Two Years in the Jungle (1885), "The
Animallai Hills! How my nerves
tingle and my pulse quickens as
I write the name!"

KEY SPECIES

MAMMALS Asian Elephant, Tiger, **Nilgiri
Langur** (*above*), Lion-tailed Macaque,
Slender Loris, Nilgiri Tahr, Gaur (Indian
Bison), Leopard, Wild Dog (Dhole),
Leopard-cat, Striped-necked Mongoose,
Brown Mongoose, Indian Giant Squirrel,
Small Travancore Flying Squirrel, Grizzled
Giant Squirrel, Mouse Deer
BIRDS RAPTORS Crested Serpent Eagle,
Black Eagle, Crested Goshawk, Rufous-
bellied Eagle, Jerdon's Baza, Mountain
Hawk Eagle, Besra, Peregrine Falcon,
Spot-bellied Eagle Owl
WOODLAND/SCRUB Grey Junglefowl,
Painted Bush Quail, Red Spurfowl, Sri
Lanka Frogmouth, Great Hornbill, Malabar
Pied Hornbill, Malabar Grey Hornbill,
White-bellied Woodpecker, Alpine Swift,
Brown-backed Needletail, Mountain
Imperial Pigeon, Nilgiri Wood Pigeon,
Dollarbird, Malabar Trogon, Asian Fairy
Bluebird, Blue-bearded Bee-eater, White-
bellied Treepie, White-bellied Shortwing,
Wynaad Laughingthrush, Hill Myna,
Nilgiri Flycatcher

Additional information on page 139

ERAVIKULAM NATIONAL PARK

Endless acres of tea plantations have altered the original habitat of the
High Ranges, along the southern tract of the Western Ghats, leaving
pristine forest only on steep slopes and in deep valleys. The Eravikulam
National Park is a dramatic, wind-swept wilderness 15 km north of
Munnar, the picturesque centre for the tea industry. The park harbours the
largest surviving, and indeed half the world's population of the endangered
Nilgiri Tahr. Yet, the stark beauty of the high mountains, rolling grass-hills
and dense evergreen *shola* forests dominates any visit to Eravikulam.

Formerly a game-hunting area, Eravikulam National Park extends over
97 sq km in Rajamalai Hills in Kerala's Idukki district. The park's altitude
ranges between 1,400 m and a high of 2,695 m, which is the elevation of
Anaimudi, peninsular India's highest peak. The park experiences very
heavy rainfall and its uninterrupted *shola*-grassland ecosystem is
unparalleled in the region of the Western Ghats and related hills.

The area has had a chequered history. Known as Hamilton's Plateau in
the late 19th century, much of this terrain was owned by the North
Travancore Land Planting Society. Later, the Kannan Devan Hill Produce

In the misty, craggy world of Eravikulam, the Nilgiri Tahr finds a secure home.

Corporation managed it as a private
hunting reserve as the area was
found unsuitable for tea plantations.
Post-1895, the High Range Game
Preservation Association ensured
the safety of much of this lush
wilderness. The region of Rajamalai
was declared a wildlife sanctuary
way back in 1936, but the present
sanctuary, which was established by
the Kerala government, did not
come into being until 1975. It was
upgraded to a national park three
years later, in recognition of its vital
ecological value.

   Eravikulam's formidable range
of attractions includes the
spectacular mass flowering of the
kurunj shrub. The herds of tahr are
very comfortable on steep slopes.
In order to view some of its other
wildlife, it is necessary to venture
deep into the park. The trek to the
foot of Anaimudi Hill will reveal
Asian Elephant, Gaur, Lion-tailed
Macaque, Leopard, giant squirrels
and, perhaps, a tiger. The nearly
100 species of birds include the
Rufous-bellied Eagle and the
Black-and-orange Flycatcher, which
can be found only in restricted
areas of south-west India. Day visits
are possible to Eravikulam for its
awe-inspiring scenery and 600-
strong tahr population. These
nimble-footed creatures are a major
attraction and they can almost
invariably be sighted at close
quarters near Rajamalai, the main
entrance situated in the tourism
zone of the park.

KEY SPECIES

MAMMALS Nilgiri Tahr, Nilgiri Langur,
Lion-tailed Macaque, Asian Elephant, Gaur
(Indian Bison), Tiger, Leopard, Wild Dog
(Dhole), Rusty Spotted Cat, Small Indian
Civet, **Striped-necked Mongoose** (*above*),
Brown Mongoose, Clawless Otter,
Common Otter, Large Brown Flying
Squirrel, Grizzled Giant Squirrel, Mouse
Deer, Sambar, Barking Deer
BIRDS RAPTORS Black Eagle, Crested
Goshawk, Rufous-bellied Eagle, Black Baza,
Mountain Hawk Eagle, Crested Serpent
Eagle, Peregrine Falcon, Pallid Harrier,
Spot-bellied Eagle Owl
WOODLAND/SCRUB Grey Junglefowl,
Painted Bush Quail, Red Spurfowl, Sri
Lanka Frogmouth, Malabar Pied Hornbill,
Alpine Swift, Malabar Trogon, Malabar
Parakeet, Asian Fairy Bluebird, Nilgiri
Wood Pigeon, Mountain Imperial Pigeon,
Spangled Drongo, Malabar Whistling
Thrush, Malabar Lark, Nilgiri Pipit, Rufous
Babbler, Grey-breasted Laughingthrush,
White-bellied Shortwing, Hill Myna, Black
Bulbul, Black-and-orange Flycatcher,
Nilgiri Flycatcher, Little Spiderhunter

Additional information on page 139

PERIYAR TIGER RESERVE

Kerala, promoted as God's own country, hosts the finest site for viewing the Asian Elephant. The Periyar Tiger Reserve, in the southernmost reaches of the Western Ghats, sprawls over 777 sq km with a core area of 350 sq km. Its foremost attraction is the rambling Periyar Lake that, despite submerging some prime forest, turned out to be a blessing in disguise for its wildlife. The lake was formed when the Periyar River was dammed in 1895 in an irrigation project to provide water to the arid regions in the east. The project was later upgraded into a full-fledged hydroelectric plant.

It is claimed that this gigantic project caused minimal damage to the wilderness. A few years after its completion, a large tract was demarcated as a reserved forest. In the 1930s, the lake and the nearby forests were declared a sanctuary. Finally, in 1977, Periyar came under Project Tiger. The hills and valleys of Periyar are covered with mixed-deciduous forest, generously touched by evergreen trees and interspersed by grasslands. The lake is shored mostly by dense tall forest and covers about 50 sq km when the water level is at its highest. Ghostly stumps of trees can be glimpsed

Nowhere but in Periyar can the lordly Asian Elephant be observed with ease and regularity.

through the winter mists as they jut out of the dark waters, often capped by some large waterbirds.

The ideal time to visit Periyar is from October to April. Herds of elephants can easily be seen while occasionally a solitary tusker emerges from the tall curtain of forest. Slow-moving boats are perfect for viewing these dawdling creatures. Sometimes Gaur is sighted at the water's edge together with Sambar, Spotted Deer, Wild Boar and otters. A pack of wild dogs can set off a flurry of activity. Very few visitors have had the good fortune to see a tiger emerging into the open for a drink.

Giant squirrels and the Nilgiri Langur are often seen in the forest canopy. There are nearly 280 species of birds, but from a boat the woodland birds would be more audible than visible. Cormorants, darters, storks, kingfishers and other waterbirds are easier to see on the lake. Excellent walking routes around Thekkady provide insights into the dense jungle and better views of the woodland birds.

Amongst the plethora of problems to be tackled by the park management at Periyar are the spreading spice plantations, livestock grazing and forest fires. The reserve is a very popular destination, averaging a quarter of a million visitors each year. The Sabarimala Ayyappan Temple in the western part of the reserve is a major draw.

KEY SPECIES

MAMMALS Asian Elephant, Tiger, Leopard, Wild Dog (Dhole), Gaur (Indian Bison), Nilgiri Langur, **Lion-tailed Macaque** (*below*), Sambar, Barking Deer, Small Indian Civet, Striped-necked Mongoose, Indian Giant Squirrel, Large Brown Flying Squirrel, Slender Loris, Common Otter
BIRDS RAPTORS Osprey, Grey-headed Fish Eagle, Rufous-bellied Eagle, Crested Goshawk, Black Baza, Besra, Brown Fish Owl, Brown Hawk Owl
WOODLAND/SCRUB Grey Junglefowl, Painted Bush Quail, Red Spurfowl, Great-eared Nightjar, Sri Lanka Frogmouth, **Great Hornbill** (*above*), Malabar Pied Hornbill, White-bellied Woodpecker, Malabar Parakeet, Dollarbird, Malabar Trogon, White-bellied Treepie, Chestnut-headed Bee-eater, Wynaad Laughingthrush
WATERSIDE Great Cormorant, Darter, Woolly-necked Stork, Pied Kingfisher

Additional information on page 140

POINT CALIMERE WILDLIFE SANCTUARY & VEDANTHANGAL WILDLIFE SANCTUARY

A giant nose of the Coromandel Coast projects into the sea a little over 300 km south of Chennai in Tamil Nadu. At the very tip of this vast swampy tract is Point Calimere, the scene of one of India's greatest avian spectacles. Declared a sanctuary in 1967, Point Calimere encompasses 17.26 sq km of sandy coast fringed by shrinking saline swamps and thorny scrub around the tidal creeks. Between October and March, it is crammed with a great variety of birds – terns, gulls, storks, herons and enormous congregations of coastal waders, but the most spectacular are the Lesser and the Greater Flamingos. On a chosen day in winter, huge waves of these lanky birds swoop down, splashing the dull colours of the landscape with their vivid pink and gleaming white.

The endangered Blackbuck, the only Indian antelope, inhabits the open coastal scrubland of Point Calimere with a population of at least a thousand. Frequently seen here are also Jackal, Wild Boar and Black-naped Hare, besides several other mammals. Dolphins and Dugong,

An explosion of waterfowl (above) *typifies Point Calimere, which is a mix of tidal swamp, coastal lagoon, scrub, thorn jungle and sandy coast* (facing page).

or Sea-cow, have been sighted and small numbers of Olive Ridley Turtles are known to nest here.

The easy sighting of birds in a mix of habitats adds to the appeal of Point Calimere. There are reportedly more than 250 avifaunal species in this sanctuary. Walking on the raised embankments provides good sightings and helps maintain a comfortable distance from the birds. Boat-rides facilitate bird-watching in some parts.

Thanjavur, just 90 km away, was the seat of the celebrated Chola kings from the 10th to the early 14th centuries. Its famous medieval temple architecture provides a break from the wildlife.

The Blackbuck in Point Calimere.

Just 40 km inland from the Coromandel Coast and 82 km south of Chennai, is one of India's smallest reserves and the oldest waterbird sanctuary. As long ago as 1798, the village folk convinced the authorities

to give protection to the birds of the 0.30 sq km area of the Vedanthangal tank. They had realized the value of the nesting birds whose droppings fertilized the water they used for irrigation.

The rain-fed Vedanthangal tank is dry through much of the summer. An earthen embankment along its western precincts impounds the water when the tank begins to fill in August. It then attracts multitudes of herons, egrets, storks, ibises and spoonbills. The *Barringtonia* trees at the edges and the centre of the tank are scenes of hectic activity. If the monsoon is heavy, these trees can be partially submerged. Their crowns, looking like leafy green islands in the water, serve as nesting platforms and perch-sites. Despite its compact size, Vedanthangal is worth a visit, especially between October and January, for the experience of seeing nesting birds in the thousands within close range.

KEY SPECIES (POINT CALIMERE)

MAMMALS Blackbuck, Jungle Cat, Wild Boar, Jackal, Striped Hyena, Spotted Deer (Chital), Bonnet Macaque, Black-naped Hare, Common Indian Mongoose

BIRDS RAPTORS White-bellied Sea Eagle, Montagu's Harrier, White-eyed Buzzard, Peregrine Falcon, Common Kestrel, Osprey **SCRUB/OPEN AREAS** Blue-faced Malkoha, Pied Cuckoo, Blue-tailed Bee-eater, Yellow-billed Babbler, Chestnut-tailed Starling, Asian Paradise-flycatcher **WATERSIDE** Greater Flamingo, **Lesser Flamingo** (*above*), Spot-billed Pelican, Great Cormorant, Grey Heron, Purple Heron, Western Reef Egret, Eurasian Spoonbill, Northern Shoveler, Red-crested Pochard, Eurasian Oystercatcher, Eurasian Curlew, Spoon-billed Sandpiper, Black-tailed Godwit, Asian Dowitcher, Pallas's Gull, Caspian Tern, Great Crested Tern, Black-capped Kingfisher

KEY SPECIES (VEDANTHANGAL)

MAMMALS Jungle Cat, Wild Boar, Black-naped Hare, Striped Hyena, Jackal **BIRDS RAPTORS** Short-toed Eagle, Eurasian Marsh Harrier, Shikra, Greater Spotted Eagle, Brahminy Kite, Black Kite **WATERSIDE** Great Cormorant, Darter, Asian Openbill, Painted Stork, Eurasian Spoonbill, Spot-billed Pelican, Comb Duck, Black-headed Ibis, Northern Shoveler

A Painted Stork flies to its nesting site near the village pond at Vedanthangal.

Additional information on page 141

APPENDIX

FACT FILE

INTERNET DISCUSSION GROUPS

WILDLIFE & CONSERVATION ORGANIZATIONS

FACT FILE

Unless specified otherwise, all accommodation inside the reserve and forest rest-houses outside are managed by the forest department. These rest-houses offer basic amenities and prior bookings are mandatory (See Contact). *The sites listed under* Wildlife Areas Nearby *are within 250 km of the reserve. The* Open Season *in some reserves may vary according to the weather conditions.*

Entry Fee *At many reserves the entry fee for Indians is between Rs 2 and Rs 25. For foreign nationals it varies from Rs 10 to Rs 200.*

Other Charges *At several reserves the entry fee is inclusive of the still camera charge. The video camera charge ranges from Rs 200 to Rs 500 per entry, but it is advisable to check with the local forest office for the current rates. Extra charges are levied for the various rides in the reserves.*

Abbreviations *APTDC (Andhra Pradesh Tourism Development Corporation), GMVN (Garhwal Mandal Vikas Nigam), HPTDC (Himachal Pradesh Tourism Development Corporation), KMVN (Kumaon Mandal Vikas Nigam), KSTDC (Karnataka State Tourism Development Corporation), KTDC (Kerala Tourism Development Corporation), MTDC (Maharashtra Tourism Development Corporation), OTDC (Orissa Tourism Development Corporation), RTDC (Rajasthan Tourism Development Corporation), WBTDC (West Bengal Tourism Development Corporation).*

Maps *The maps are not to scale and have a north orientation. Information on tiger reserves is from* Project Tiger Status Report 2001, *Ministry of Environment and Forests, Government of India.*

WATER		CORE AREA		ROAD, TRAIL	FORT
WETLAND		MULTI-USE AREA	+++ RAILWAY		REST-HOUSE
SANCTUARY		BOUNDARY		CANAL	MOUNTAINS

NORTHERN ZONE

DACHIGAM NATIONAL PARK
Check latest security situation before proceeding

1 Draphama
2 Pahlipora
3 Gratnar
4 Hoksar
5 Sangargulu
6 Marsar Lake
7 Main gate

CONTACT Wildlife Warden, c/o Chief Wildlife Warden, Jammu and Kashmir State, 1st Floor, Tourist Reception Centre, Srinagar 190001, Jammu and Kashmir Tel (0194) 492627 Fax 572570

AREA 141 sq km

DISTANCE From main gate to: Srinagar 22 km (airport 30 km), Jammu 312 km

ACCOMMODATION
 Inside the reserve Forest rest-houses, inspection huts and dormitories in Lower Dachigam; inspection huts and camping sites in Upper Dachigam
 Outside the reserve
  Srinagar (STD code 0194)
  Houseboats on Dal Lake, 15 km from Dachigam's main gate
  Broadway, Tel 459001-03 Fax 459004
  Centaur Lake View, Tel 475632 Fax 471877
  Grand Palace Intercontinental, Tel 470101, 456701 Fax 453794
  Metro, Tel 477126 Fax 478256

OPEN SEASON
 Upper Dachigam Mid-April to October
 Lower Dachigam Throughout the year

BEST TIME TO VISIT
Upper Dachigam June to August
Lower Dachigam May to June,
mid-September to November
CLIMATE
Upper Dachigam
April to October 7°C–21°C
Lower Dachigam
April to October 9°C–30°C
November to March -3°C–15°C
WILDLIFE AREAS NEARBY
Hokersar Wildlife Sanctuary
Contact See Dachigam National Park
Distance Srinagar 10 km
Best time to visit September to November
Mammals Red Fox, Common Otter
Birds Mallard, Greylag Goose, Northern
Shoveler, Bar-headed Goose
Overa Wildlife Sanctuary
Contact See Dachigam National Park
Tel (0194) 452469
Distance Pahalgam 11 km, Srinagar
78 km, Dachigam's main gate 100 km
Best time to visit April to June,
September to October
Mammals Hangul (Kashmir Stag),
Himalayan Black Bear, Brown Bear,
Musk Deer, Yellow-throated Marten
Birds Himalayan Monal, Koklass
Pheasant, Lammergeier

HEMIS NATIONAL PARK
Check latest security situation before proceeding
CONTACT Wildlife Warden, Badami Bagh, Leh,
Ladakh 194101, Jammu and Kashmir
Telefax (01982) 52171. Due to minimal
infrastructure in the park, it is advisable
to contact tour operators in Leh, Srinagar
or Delhi for visits
AREA 4,100 sq km
DISTANCE From Hemis Gompa: Thiksey 25 km,
Stok 25 km, Shey 30 km, Leh 42 km,
Manali 450 km, Srinagar airport 464 km
ACCOMMODATION
Inside the reserve No forest rest-houses,
but camping sites available
Outside the reserve Hemis Gompa and

basic guest-houses at Hemis village
and Karu (open only during summer);
guest-houses at Thiksey and Shey
Leh (STD code 01982)
Buddha Garden, Tel 44074
Dragon, Tel 52139 Fax 52720
Email advnorth@vsnl.com
Ga-Ldan, Tel 52173 Fax 53330
Gypsy's Panorama Hotel, Tel 52660
Khangri, Tel 52311
K-Sar Palace, Tel 52348
Mandala, Tel 52330
Milarepa, Tel 53218
Omasila, Tel 52119
ShambhaLa, Tel 52607 Telefax 51100
Singge Palace, Tel 53344 Fax 52042
Yak Tail, Tel 52118
Stok Tiger Tops Ladakh Sarai, [Delhi Tel
(011) 3671055, 3511483 Fax 3677483]
OPEN SEASON Mid-May to October
BEST TIME TO VISIT June to August
CLIMATE May to July 4°C–34°C
August to October -3°C–23°C
WILDLIFE AREAS NEARBY
*Advisable to check with travel agents in Leh
for transport to lakes and camping permission*
Pangong Tso
Distance Leh 90 km
Best time to visit Mid-May to October
Mammals Snow Leopard (Ounce),
Tibetan Wild Ass, Ibex
Birds Black-necked Crane, Ruddy
Shelduck, Bar-headed Goose
Tso Kar
Distance Leh 105 km
Best time to visit Mid-May to October
Mammals Snow Leopard (Ounce),
Bharal (Blue Sheep), Ibex
Birds Black-necked Crane, Ruddy
Shelduck, Bar-headed Goose,
Brown-headed Gull
Tso Moriri
Distance Leh 160 km
Best time to visit Mid-May to October
Mammals Snow Leopard (Ounce), Ibex
Birds Ruddy Shelduck, Bar-headed
Goose, Brown-headed Gull

GREAT HIMALAYAN NATIONAL PARK
Entry permits required

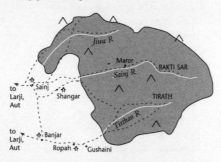

CONTACT Director, Great Himalayan National
Park, Shamshi, District Kullu 175126,
Himachal Pradesh Telefax (01902) 65320
Email dirchnp@sancharnet.in

AREA 754.40 sq km

DISTANCE From Gushaini to: Aut 30 km,
Bhuntar 45 km, Kullu 55 km,
Mandi 70 km, Manali 95 km
From Sainj to: Aut 15 km, Kullu 50 km

ACCOMMODATION

Inside the reserve Patrolling huts and
camping sites

Outside the reserve Forest rest-houses at
Aut, Bandal, Ropah, Sainj and Shangar;
Public Works Department (PWD) rest-
houses at Banjar, Bathad and Larji.
Permission required from PWD office:
Executive Engineer, Kullu Division No II,
Kullu 175101, Himachal Pradesh

Bhuntar (STD code 01902)
Noble Guest House, Tel 65077
Sunbeam, Tel 65790
Trans Shiva, Tel 65623

Kullu (STD code 01902)
Apple Valley Resort, Tel 66266
Aroma Classic, Tel 23075
Hotel Sarvari (HPTDC), Tel 22471
New Vikrant, Tel 22756
Rock-n-River, Tel 24214
Shobla, Tel 22800

OPEN SEASON September to early June

BEST TIME TO VISIT April to early June,
September to October

CLIMATE September to October 8°C–22°C
November to February -4°C–15°C
March to June 7°C–27°C

WILDLIFE AREAS NEARBY

Manali Wildlife Sanctuary
Contact Divisional Forest Officer
(Wildlife), Kullu Division, Kullu 175101,
Himachal Pradesh Tel (01902) 22276
Distance Manali 4 km
Best time to visit April to June,
mid-September to November
Mammals Musk Deer, Himalayan Tahr,
Serow, Himalayan Palm Civet
Birds Himalayan Monal, Western
Tragopan, Cheer Pheasant

Chail Wildlife Sanctuary
Contact Divisional Forest Officer
(Wildlife), Shimla Division, Talland,
Shimla 171001, Himachal Pradesh
Tel (0177) 223993
Distance Shimla 45 km, Kullu 245 km
Best time to visit April to June,
September to November
Mammals Himalayan Tahr, Goral,
Leopard, Yellow-throated Marten
Birds Cheer Pheasant, Yellow-billed Blue
Magpie, Lammergeier

Shimla Water Catchment Wildlife Sanctuary
Contact See Chail Wildlife Sanctuary
Distance Shimla 11 km
Best time to visit April to June,
September to November
Mammals Himalayan Black Bear,
Yellow-throated Marten, Serow
Birds Himalayan Monal, Koklass
Pheasant, Spotted Nutcracker

VALLEY OF FLOWERS NATIONAL PARK

CONTACT Divisional Forest Officer, Nanda
Devi Biosphere Reserve, Joshimath,
District Chamoli 246443, Uttaranchal
Tel (01389) 22179

AREA 87.50 sq km

DISTANCE From Ghangaria (base camp) to:
Valley of Flowers National Park 5 km,
Govindghat 13 km, Joshimath 33 km,
Badrinath 38 km, Rishikesh 298 km

Nilgiri Parbat

Rataban

Glacier

Nar Parbat

3
4   5
6
2

to ◄
Badrinath   1   Gauri
Parbat

Ghangaria   Hemkund   Saptsring
Bhyundhar

Govindghat
to Joshimath

1 Paira   4 Sewachand
2 Lower Nagtal   5 Tipra Kharak
3 Bamini Dhaur   6 Kunt Khal

ACCOMMODATION
  Inside the reserve Camping is prohibited
  inside the national park limits
  Outside the reserve
    Ghangaria A forest rest-house;
    GMVN tourist rest-house and
    tent accommodation, GMVN
    Dehradun Tel (0135) 749308
    Fax 744408; a large *gurudwara* with
    basic amenities
    Joshimath (STD code 01389)
    GMVN rest-house, Tel 22226
    Shailja Hotel, Tel 22208
OPEN SEASON April to October
BEST TIME TO VISIT July to August
CLIMATE April to June 10°C–23°C
    July to October 7°C–22°C
WILDLIFE AREAS NEARBY
  Nanda Devi National Park
    Contact See Valley of Flowers
    National Park
    Distance Joshimath 23 km,
    Rishikesh 275 km
    Best time to visit April to October
    Mammals Snow Leopard (Ounce),
    Musk Deer, Serow, Bharal (Blue Sheep),
    Brown Bear
    Birds Himalayan Monal, Koklass
    Pheasant, Golden Eagle
  Kedarnath Wildlife Sanctuary
    Contact Divisional Forest Officer,
    Kedarnath Wildlife Division, Gopeshwar,
    Chamoli 246401, Uttaranchal

Tel (01372) 52149
Distance Gopeshwar 4 km, Soneprayag
20 km, Rishikesh 210 km
Best time to visit April to October
Mammals Snow Leopard (Ounce), Musk
Deer, Serow, Himalayan Tahr
Birds Himalayan Monal, Kalij Pheasant

RAJAJI NATIONAL PARK

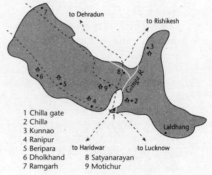

to Dehradun   to Rishikesh

7
3
8
6
5
9
4
Ganga R.
1
2

Laldhang

1 Chilla gate
2 Chilla
3 Kunnao
4 Ranipur
5 Beripara   to Haridwar   to Lucknow
6 Dholkhand
7 Ramgarh   8 Satyanarayan
                 9 Motichur

CONTACT Director, Rajaji National Park,
    5/1 Ansari Marg, Dehradun 248001,
    Uttaranchal Tel (0135) 621669
AREA 820 sq km
DISTANCE From Chilla gate to:
    Haridwar 10 km, Rishikesh 12 km,
    Dehradun airport 32 km, Delhi 200 km
ACCOMMODATION
  Inside the reserve Several forest rest-
  houses in Beripara, Chilla, Dholkhand,
  Kunnao, Motichur and Ranipur
  Outside the reserve
    Chilla GMVN tourist rest-house,
      Tel (01382) 66678, 66697
    Haridwar (STD code 0133)
    Ashok, Tel 427328
    Kailash, Tel 427789
    Mansarovar International, Tel 426501
    Midtown, Tel 427507 Fax 426049
    Neelkanth, Tel 428384
    Rahi Motel Tourist Bungalow (GMVN),
      Tel 428686, 420642
    Sagar Ganga Resort, Tel 422115
    Suvidha Deluxe, Tel 427423

Rishikesh (STD code 01364)
Akash Ganga, Tel 430870 Fax 432600
Baseraa, Tel 430720, 430767 Fax 433106
Ganga View, Tel 430781 Fax 431081
Himalaya, Tel 434990, 432331
Mandakini International, Tel 430781
  [Delhi Tel (011) 5754113]
New Tourist Rest-house (GMVN),
  Tel 433002
Rishilok Tourist Rest-house (GMVN),
  Tel 430373
Shikhar, Tel 433817, 434709
Dehradun (STD code 0135)
Ajanta Continental, Tel 749595-97
  Fax 747722
Gaurab, Tel 654215
Great Value, Tel 742731, 744086
  Fax 746058
Hotel Drona (GMVN), Tel 654371
  [Main office Tel 749308 Fax 744408]
Madhuban, Tel 744307, 749990
  Fax 746496
Meedo, Tel 627088
Motel Kwality, Tel 657001-02
President, Tel 657386, 657082
  Fax 658883
White House, Tel 652765
OPEN SEASON October to June
BEST TIME TO VISIT November to March
CLIMATE October to February 5°C–29°C
  March to June 15°C–40°C

CORBETT TIGER RESERVE

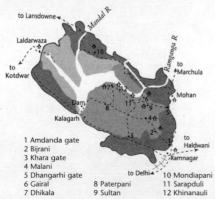

to Lansdowne
Mandal R
Laldarwaza
to Kotdwar
Ramganga R
to Marchula
Mohan
Dam
Kalagarh
to Delhi
to Haldwani
Ramnagar

1 Amdanda gate
2 Bijrani
3 Khara gate
4 Malani
5 Dhangarhi gate
6 Gairal
7 Dhikala
8 Paterpani
9 Sultan
10 Mondiapani
11 Sarapduli
12 Khinanauli

CONTACT Field Director, Corbett Tiger
  Reserve, P O Ramnagar, District Nainital
  244715, Uttaranchal
  Tel (05947) 51489 Fax 51376
AREA 1,318.54 sq km
DISTANCE From Dhangarhi gate to:
  Garjia 10 km, Kumeria 12 km,
  Ramnagar 19 km, Dhikala tourist
  complex 30 km, Nainital 85 km,
  Delhi 260 km
ACCOMMODATION
Inside the reserve Forest rest-houses at
  Bijrani, Gairal, Kanda, Khinanauli, Malani,
  Mondiapani, Sarapduli and Sultan;
  a tourist complex at Dhikala
Outside the reserve
Garjia (STD code 05947)
  Claridges Corbett Hideaway, Tel 85959
    [Delhi Tel (011) 3010211]
  Corbett Riverside Resort, Tel 85960-61
    Fax 85960
  Infinity Resorts (formerly Tiger Tops),
    Tel 51279-80 Fax 51880 [Delhi Tel
    (011) 6691209 Fax 6691219; Mumbai
    Tel (022) 2350100 Fax 2350277]
    Email kil@varunship.com
Kumeria Quality Inn, Tel (05946) 85520
    Telefax 85230
Ramnagar (STD code 05947)
  Govind Hotel, Tel 85615
  Hotel Everest, Tel 85099
  KMVN tourist complex, Tel 51225
OPEN SEASON October to early June
BEST TIME TO VISIT December to April
CLIMATE October to November 12°C–30°C
  December to February 3°C–25°C
  March to June 12°C–38°C

DUDHWA TIGER RESERVE

CONTACT Field Director and Conservator
  (Forests), Project Tiger, Dudhwa Tiger
  Reserve, District Lakhimpur-Kheri
  262701, Uttar Pradesh
  Telefax (05872) 52106
AREA 884.00 sq km
DISTANCE From main gate to: Palia 10 km,
  Lucknow 220 km

SARISKA TIGER RESERVE

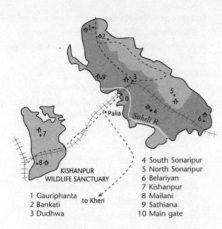

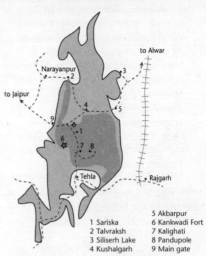

4 South Sonaripur
5 North Sonaripur
6 Belariyan
7 Kishanpur
8 Mailani
9 Sathiana
10 Main gate

1 Gauriphanta
2 Bankati
3 Dudhwa

to Kheri

KISHANPUR
WILDLIFE SANCTUARY

5 Akbarpur
6 Kankwadi Fort
7 Kalighati
8 Pandupole
9 Main gate

1 Sariska
2 Talvraksh
3 Siliserh Lake
4 Kushalgarh

ACCOMMODATION

Inside the reserve Forest rest-houses, log huts and a dormitory at Dudhwa; forest rest-houses at Bankati, Belariyan, Gauriphanta, North and South Sonaripur, Sathiana, and at Kishanpur and Mailani

Outside the reserve

Palia (STD code 05871)

Basera, Tel 33433

Mahendra, Tel 33264

Mor, Tel 33424

Tiger Haven, Tel 33978

OPEN SEASON October to early June

BEST TIME TO VISIT Early December to March

CLIMATE October to November 12˚C–32˚C
December to February 4˚C–27˚C
March to June 15˚C–40˚C

WILDLIFE AREAS NEARBY

Katerniaghat Wildlife Sanctuary

Contact Divisional Forest Officer, Katerniaghat Wildlife Division, Bahraich, Uttar Pradesh Tel (05252) 32498

Distance Nanpara 40 km, Dudhwa 100 km, Lucknow 200 km

Best time to visit November to March

Mammals Swamp Deer (Barasingha), Tiger, Sloth Bear

Reptiles Gharial, Mugger (Marsh Crocodile), Yellow Monitor

Birds Ruddy Shelduck, Black-necked Stork, Black Stork, Red Junglefowl

CONTACT Field Director, Project Tiger, Sariska Tiger Reserve, P O Sariska, District Alwar 301001, Rajasthan Tel (0144) 41333

AREA 866.00 sq km

DISTANCE From main gate to: Alwar 35 km, Jaipur 110 km, Delhi 180 km

ACCOMMODATION

Inside the reserve

A forest rest-house at Sariska

Outside the reserve

Sariska (STD code 0146)

Hotel Sariska Palace, Tel 524247

Hotel Tiger Den (RTDC), *near the main gate*, Tel 41342

Siliserh (STD code 0144)

Hill Fort Kesroli, Tel 81312 [Delhi Tel (011) 4616145 Fax 4621112]

Lake Palace Hotel (RTDC), Tel 86322

Alwar (STD code 0144)

Alwar, Tel 20012 Fax 332250

Aravali, Tel 332883 Fax 332011

Meenal Hotel (RTDC), Tel 22852

OPEN SEASON October to June

BEST TIME TO VISIT December to March

CLIMATE October to November 16˚C–34˚C
December to February 4˚C–28˚C
March to June 18˚C–42˚C

WILDLIFE AREAS NEARBY

Tal Chhapper Wildlife Sanctuary

Contact Wildlife Office, Van Bhavan,
Vaniki Path, Jaipur 302005, Rajasthan
Tel (0141) 380382 Fax 380496

Distance Jaipur 175 km

Best time to visit November to March

Mammals Blackbuck, Chinkara (Indian
Gazelle), Wolf

Reptiles Sand Boa, Desert Monitor

Birds Short-toed Eagle, Steppe Eagle,
Demoiselle Crane, Cream-coloured
Courser, Painted Sandgrouse

KEOLADEO GHANA NATIONAL PARK (BHARATPUR BIRD SANCTUARY)

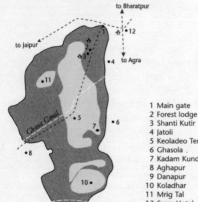

1 Main gate
2 Forest lodge
3 Shanti Kutir
4 Jatoli
5 Keoladeo Temple
6 Ghasola
7 Kadam Kund
8 Aghapur
9 Danapur
10 Koladhar
11 Mrig Tal
12 Saras Hotel

CONTACT Deputy Chief Wildlife Warden/Park
Director, Keoladeo Ghana National Park,
Bharatpur 321001, Rajasthan
Tel (05644) 22777 Fax 22864

AREA 28.73 sq km

DISTANCE From main gate to: Bharatpur
railway station 5 km, Agra 55 km,
Delhi 180 km, Jaipur 178 km

ACCOMMODATION

Inside the reserve

Shanti Kutir, a forest rest-house, about
2 km from main gate
ITDC (Indian Tourism Development
Corporation) forest lodge,
Tel (05644) 22760

Outside the reserve

Bharatpur (STD code 05644)
Several guest-houses, hotels and camping
sites within 5 km of the park's main gate
Crane Crib, Tel 24224
Eagle's Nest, Tel 25144
Falcon Guest House, Tel 23815
Jungle Lodge, Tel 25622
Laxmi Vilas Palace, Tel 23523
   Fax 25259
Paradise, Tel 23791
Park Palace, Tel 23783, 23222
Pelican, Tel 24221
Pratap Palace, Tel 24245, 25144
Sangam, Tel 25616
Saras Hotel (RTDC), Tel 23700
Spoonbill, Tel 23571
Sunbird, Tel 25701

OPEN SEASON Throughout the year

BEST TIME TO VISIT
July to October (nesting waterbirds),
November to February (wintering birds)

CLIMATE March to June 16°C–41°C
July to October 20°C–40°C
November to February 4°C–28°C

WILDLIFE AREAS NEARBY

Sambhar Lake (salt-water lake)

Distance Jaipur 90 km

Best time to visit October to March

Mammals Nilgai (Blue Bull), Chinkara
(Indian Gazelle)

Birds Greater Flamingo, Lesser Flamingo,
Demoiselle Crane, Common Crane,
Great White Pelican, Steppe Eagle

Sultanpur National Park

Contact Divisional Inspector, Wildlife,
Sultanpur National Park, District
Gurgaon, c/o DFO (Terr.) Gurgaon
122001, Haryana Tel (0124) 6322057

Distance Delhi 48 km

Best time to visit October to March

Mammals Nilgai (Blue Bull), Jackal,
Indian Fox, Jungle Cat

Birds Common Crane, Bar-headed
Goose, Ruddy Shelduck, Painted Stork,
Great White Pelican, Greater Spotted
Eagle, Osprey

WESTERN ZONE

DESERT NATIONAL PARK

Permission required for visiting fenced enclosures

CONTACT Deputy Conservator of Forests,
Desert National Park, Jaisalmer 345001,
Rajasthan Tel (02992) 52489
Fax 52201, 52063

AREA 3,162.00 sq km

DISTANCE From Sudasari enclosure to: Sam
15 km, Jaisalmer 55 km, Jodhpur 370 km

ACCOMMODATION

Inside the reserve Forest rest-houses at
several locations

Outside the reserve

Sam Hotel Sam Dhani (RTDC), contact
Jaisalmer's Hotel Moomal for bookings

Jaisalmer (STD code 02992)
Dhola Maru, Tel 52863 Fax 53124
Gorbandh Palace, Tel 51511 Fax 52749
Himmatgarh Palace, Tel 52002
Hotel Moomal (RTDC), Tel 52392
Jaisal Castle, Tel 52362
Jaisal Palace, Tel 52717 Fax 50257
Jawahar Niwas Palace, Tel 52208
Fax 52611
Mandir Palace, Tel 52788
Narayan Niwas Palace, Tel 52408
Fax 52101
Paradise, Tel 52674
Rang Mahal, Tel 50907 Fax 51305
[Shimla Tel (0177) 53061]

OPEN SEASON Throughout the year

BEST TIME TO VISIT December to March

CLIMATE March to June 18°C–42°C
July to October 20°C–38°C
November to February 3°C–29°C

WILDLIFE AREAS NEARBY

Wood Fossil Park (180 million-year-old
tree fossils)

Contact Jaisalmer tourist office,
Tel (02992) 52406

Distance Jaisalmer 15 km

Best time to visit November to March

Mammals Chinkara (Indian Gazelle),
Blackbuck, Jackal

Reptiles Sand Boa, Black Cobra,
Desert Monitor, Spiny-tailed Lizard

Birds Long-legged Buzzard, Imperial
Eagle, Spotted Sandgrouse

Khichan (congregation site of the
Demoiselle Crane)

Distance Phalodi 10 km,
Jaisalmer *about* 160 km

Best time to visit November to February

Mammals Chinkara (Indian Gazelle),
Desert Fox, Blackbuck

Reptiles Black Cobra, Yellow Monitor

Birds Demoiselle Crane, Steppe Eagle,
Imperial Eagle

WILD ASS (LITTLE RANN) WILDLIFE SANCTUARY

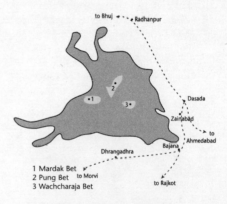

1 Mardak Bet
2 Pung Bet
3 Wachcharaja Bet

CONTACT Sanctuary Superintendent/Assistant
Conservator of Forests, Wild Ass
(Dhrangadhra) Sanctuary, Halvad Road,
Dhrangadhra, Surendranagar District
363310, Gujarat Telefax (02754) 60716,
61348 OR Bajana Range office,
Tel (02757) 26281

AREA 4,953.71 sq km

DISTANCE From Zainabad to: Dasada 10 km,
Viramgam 45 km, Dhrangadhra 58 km,
Ahmedabad 105 km

ACCOMMODATION

Outside the reserve

Zainabad Camp Zainabad, Tel (02757)
41333, 41335 Fax 41334
Email desertcoursers@hotmail.com

Dasada Rann Rider, Tel (02757) 40257
[Ahmedabad Tel (079) 6586821]
Dhrangadhra Devji Dhamecha,
Tel (02754) 80560 Fax 80300
OPEN SEASON Mid-November to June
BEST TIME TO VISIT December to March
CLIMATE November to February 4°C–32°C
March to June 14°C–44°C
WILDLIFE AREAS NEARBY
Nal Sarovar Wildlife Sanctuary
Contact Assistant Conservator of Forests,
Nal Sarovar Bird Sanctuary, At & P O
Vekaria, Tehsil Viramgam, District
Ahmedabad, Gujarat Tel (079) 2122430
Distance Ahmedabad 64 km
Best time to visit November to February
Mammals Wolf, Jackal, Striped Hyena
Reptiles Common Monitor, Rock Python
Birds Greater Flamingo, Lesser Flamingo,
Spot-billed Pelican, Great White Pelican,
Common Crane, Demoiselle Crane,
Caspian Tern, Greater Spotted Eagle

MARINE NATIONAL PARK
Entry permits required

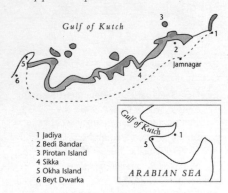

1 Jadiya
2 Bedi Bandar
3 Pirotan Island
4 Sikka
5 Okha Island
6 Beyt Dwarka

CONTACT Conservator of Forests, Marine
National Park, Ganjiwada Nagar,
Nagnath Gate Police Chowki,
Jamnagar 360001, Gujarat
Tel (0288) 552077 Fax 555336
AREA 162.89 sq km
DISTANCE From Bedi Bandar jetty to:
Jamnagar 5 km, Pirotan Island 15 km

ACCOMMODATION
Inside the reserve Basic cabins on Pirotan
Island; camping on permission
Outside the reserve
Jamnagar (STD code 0288)
Ashiana, Tel 550583
Chandramauli, Tel 672111
Dreamland, Tel 670436
President, Tel 557491-92 Fax 558491
Vishal International, Tel 553952, 555026
OPEN SEASON October to June
BEST TIME TO VISIT December to March
CLIMATE October to November 18°C–34°C
December to February 8°C–32°C
March to June 18°C–40°C
WILDLIFE AREAS NEARBY
Khijadiya Wildlife Sanctuary
Contact See Marine National Park
Distance Jamnagar 10 km
Best time to visit November to March
Birds Greater Flamingo, Lesser Flamingo,
Common Crane, Demoiselle Crane,
Eurasian Curlew, Pied Avocet

**BLACKBUCK (VELAVADAR)
NATIONAL PARK**

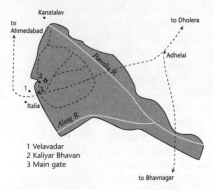

1 Velavadar
2 Kaliyar Bhavan
3 Main gate

CONTACT Assistant Conservator of Forests,
Blackbuck National Park, Velavadar, F/10,
Bahumali Bhavan, Bhavnagar 360001,
Gujarat Tel (0278) 426425 Fax 632900
AREA 34.08 sq km
DISTANCE From main gate to:
Valabhipur 31 km, Bhavnagar 64 km

ACCOMMODATION

Inside the reserve

Kaliyar Bhavan forest lodge

Outside the reserve

Bhavnagar (STD code 0278)

Apollo, Tel 425250-52 Fax 412440

Bluehill, Tel 426951-53 Fax 427313

Jubilee, Tel 430045

Nilambag Palace,Tel 424241, 429323
Fax 428072

Vrindavan, Tel 518928

White Rose, Tel 514022 Fax 413403

OPEN SEASON Throughout the year

BEST TIME TO VISIT December to March

CLIMATE March to June 18°C–42°C
July to October 21°C–35°C
November to February 7°C–30°C

GIR NATIONAL PARK

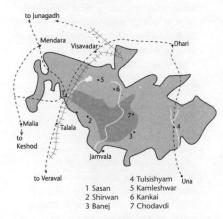

to Junagadh

Mendara

Visavadar

Dhari

•5

•6

Malia

Talala

2

7•

to
Keshod

3

4

Jamvala

to Veraval

Una

1 Sasan   4 Tulsishyam
2 Shirwan   5 Kamleshwar
3 Banej   6 Kankai
             7 Chodavdi

CONTACT Dèputy Conservator of Forests
(Wildlife Circle), Gir National Park
& Sanctuary, P O Sasan-Gir, District
Junagadh 362135, Gujarat
Tel (0285) 630051, 631678 Fax 632900

AREA 258.71 sq km

DISTANCE From Sasan to: Veraval 40 km,
Junagadh 58 km, Keshod 85 km

ACCOMMODATION

Outside the reserve

Sasan (STD code 02877)

Gir Lodge (Taj), Tel 85501-04, 85521

Fax 85528 [Mumbai Tel
(022) 2023366 Fax 2023235]
Email trn@tajhotels.com

Maneland Lodge, Tel 85555

Sinh Sadan Forest Lodge, Tel 85540

Junagadh (STD code 0285)

Ashiyana, Tel 620706

Girnar Hotel, Tel 621201

Relief, Tel 620280

Vishala, Tel 631599

OPEN SEASON Mid-October to early June

BEST TIME TO VISIT December to March

CLIMATE October to November 15°C–34°C
December to February 8°C–30°C
March to June 18°C–42°C

SANJAY GANDHI (BORIVLI) NATIONAL PARK

CONTACT Deputy Conservator of Forests,
Sanjay Gandhi National Park, Borivli
(East), Mumbai 400066, Maharashtra
Tel (022) 8860362, 8860389

AREA 86.96 sq km

DISTANCE From Borivli main gate to:
Mumbai international airport 18 km,
Mumbai (Nariman Point) 40 km

ACCOMMODATION

Inside the reserve

Forest rest-houses, bungalows, log cabins

Outside the reserve

Mumbai (STD code 022)

Juhu Hotel, Tel 6184012-15

Ramada Hotel Palm Grove, Tel 6112323

Taj Mahal Hotel, Tel 2023366

The Centaur, Tel 6156660

The Leela, Tel 8353535, 8363636

The Oberoi, Tel 2025757

The Orchid, Tel 6164040

The Resort, Tel 8820992, 8820471

Tunga International, Tel 8346666,
8366010 Fax 8366003

OPEN SEASON Throughout the year

BEST TIME TO VISIT September to October
(insects, flora and nature walks),
December to February (bird-watching)

CLIMATE March to October 18°C–36°C
November to February 12°C–31°C

WILDLIFE AREAS NEARBY
Karnala Wildlife Sanctuary
Contact Deputy Conservator of Forests
(WL) Thane, L B S Road, Naupada,
Near Highway Naka, Thane 400602,
Maharashtra Tel (022) 5402522
Distance Mumbai 70 km
Best time to visit November to March
Mammals Leopard, Barking Deer,
Common Langur
Reptiles Rock Python, Common Monitor
Birds Peregrine Falcon, Malabar
Whistling Thrush, Heart-spotted
Woodpecker, Pompadour Green Pigeon
Bhimashankar Wildlife Sanctuary
Contact Deputy Conservator of Forests
(WL) Pune, New P M T Building, 3rd Floor,
Shankarsheth Road, Swargate, Pune
411042, Maharashtra Tel (020) 4471465
Distance Pune 160 km, Mumbai 250 km
Best time to visit November to March
Mammals Leopard, Indian Giant
Squirrel, Barking Deer, Mouse Deer
Reptiles Rock Python, Russel's Viper
Birds Green Imperial Pigeon, Crested
Serpent Eagle

DANDELI WILDLIFE SANCTUARY
CONTACT Deputy Conservator of Forests,
Dandeli Wildlife Division, Dandeli, Uttar-
Kannada District 581325, Karnataka
Tel (08284) 31585
AREA 843.16 sq km
DISTANCE From main gate to: Dandeli 10 km,
Ganeshgudi 25 km, Londa 60 km, Hubli
75 km, Belgaum 105 km, Dabolim
airport 140 km, Karwar 120 km
ACCOMMODATION
Inside the reserve Six forest rest-houses
Outside the reserve
Kulgi Nature Camp, Tel (08284) 31585
Dandeli Kali Wilderness Camp (Jungle
Lodges), [Bangalore Tel (080)
5583276, 5586154 Fax 5586163]
Email junglelodge@vsnl.com
Ganeshgudi Bison River Resort (Indian
Adventures), Tel (08383) 46548

Telefax 46539 [Mumbai Tel (022)
6408742, 6433622, 6428244
Fax 6458401] Email iawr@vsnl.com
OPEN SEASON October to May
BEST TIME TO VISIT Late November to March
CLIMATE October to November 18°C–32°C
December to February 12°C–30°C
March to May 20°C–34°C
WILDLIFE AREAS NEARBY
Cotigao, Netravali and Mollem Wildlife Sanctuaries
Distance (Cotigao) Dabolim airport 75
km; (Netravali) Dabolim airport 55 km;
(Mollem) Dabolim airport 45 km
Contact Director (Wildlife & Eco-
tourism), IV Floor, Junta House, Panaji
403001, Goa Tel (0832) 229701
Best time to visit November to March
Mammals Leopard, Gaur (Indian Bison),
Spotted Deer (Chital), Sloth Bear,
Sambar, Indian Giant Squirrel
Birds Malabar Pied Hornbill, Malabar
Trogon, Asian Fairy Bluebird, Nilgiri
Wood Pigeon, Grey Junglefowl
Sharavathi Valley Wildlife Sanctuary
Contact Deputy Conservator of Forests,
Wildlife Division, D C Office Compound,
Shimoga 577201, Karnataka
Tel (08182) 22983
Distance Mangalore 185 km, Dandeli
185 km, Dabolim airport 200 km
Best time to visit December to March
Mammals Tiger, Sloth Bear, Leopard
Birds Great Hornbill, Malabar Trogon,
Rufous-bellied Eagle, Sri Lanka
Frogmouth
Ranebennur Wildlife Sanctuary
Contact Assistant Conservator of Forests,
Wildlife Sub-division, Dharwad 580001,
Karnataka Tel (0836) 440302
Distance Dandeli *about* 110 km
Best time to visit November to February
(birds and mammals), June to October
(for observing Indian Bustard)
Mammals Blackbuck, Wolf
Reptiles Common Monitor
Birds Indian Bustard, Short-eared Owl

CENTRAL ZONE

RANTHAMBORE TIGER RESERVE

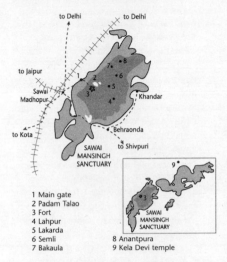

1 Main gate
2 Padam Talao
3 Fort
4 Lahpur
5 Lakarda
6 Semli
7 Bakaula
8 Anantpura
9 Kela Devi temple

CONTACT Field Director, Project Tiger,
Ranthambore Tiger Reserve, Sawai
Madhopur 322001, Rajasthan
Tel (07462) 20223, 22004 Fax 21212
AREA 1,334.64 sq km
DISTANCE From reserve's main gate to:
Sawai Madhopur 12 km, Jaipur 175 km,
Delhi 350 km
ACCOMMODATION
Inside the reserve
Overnight stay not allowed
Outside the reserve
Sawai Madhopur (STD code 07462)
Ankur Resort, Tel 20792
Anurag Resort, Tel 20451
Castle Jhoomar Baori (RTDC), Tel 20495
Hammir Wildlife Resort, Tel 20562
Fax 21842
Ranthambhor Bagh, Telefax 21728
Ranthambhor Regency, Tel 21176
Sawai Madhopur Lodge (Taj), Tel 20541,
20247 Fax 20718 [Delhi Tel (011)
3026162 Fax 3026070]
Email trn@tajhotels.com
Sherbagh, Tel 52119-20 Fax 20811

[Delhi Tel (011) 3316534 Fax 3312118]
Email sherbagh@vsnl.com
Tiger Den Resort, Tel 52070, 52085
Fax 20702
Tiger Moon Resort (Indian Adventures),
Tel 52042 [Mumbai Tel (022)
6408742, 6433622 Fax 6458401]
Email iawr@vsnl.com
Vanyavilas (Oberoi), Tel 23999 Fax 23988
[Mumbai Tel 2326051, 2326057,
2324343 Fax 2043133; Delhi Tel
(011) 4363030 Fax 4360484]
Email reservations@vanyavilas.com
Vinayak Tourist Complex (RTDC),
Tel 21333
OPEN SEASON October to June
BEST TIME TO VISIT December to April
CLIMATE October to November 15°C–32°C
December to February 4°C–25°C
March to June 16°C–42°C
WILDLIFE AREAS NEARBY
Soorwal Bunder
Distance Sawai Madhopur 22 km
Best time to visit December to March
Mammals Jackal, Indian Fox
Birds Dalmatian Pelican, Great White
Pelican, Indian Skimmer, Pallas's Gull
National Chambal Wildlife Sanctuary
Contact Divisional Forest Officer,
National Chambal Wildlife Division, Mau
Van Block, Agra 282003, Uttar Pradesh
Tel (0562) 320091
Distance Etawah 8 km, Agra 40 km
Best time to visit December to April
Mammals Gangetic Dolphin, Nilgai
(Blue Bull), Chinkara (Indian Gazelle)
Reptiles Mugger (Marsh Crocodile),
Gharial, Rock Python, Yellow Monitor
Birds Demoiselle Crane, Common Crane,
Grey-headed Fish Eagle, Indian Skimmer
Madhav (Shivpuri) National Park
Contact Director, Madhav National Park,
Shivpuri 473551, Madhya Pradesh
Tel (07492) 23379
Distance Shivpuri 5 km, Gwalior 112 km,
Sawai Madhopur 140 km
Best time to visit November to March

Mammals Tiger, Sambar, Nilgai
(Blue Bull)
Reptiles Mugger (Marsh Crocodile),
Rock Python
Birds Crested Serpent Eagle, Bonelli's
Eagle, Ruddy Shelduck

Karera Wildlife Sanctuary
Contact *See* Madhav National Park
Distance Shivpuri 45 km, Jhansi 55 km,
Sawai Madhopur *about* 175 km
Best time to visit November to March
Mammals Blackbuck, Wolf, Chinkara
(Indian Gazelle)
Reptiles Sand Boa, Common Monitor
Birds Indian Bustard, Greater Flamingo

BANDHAVGARH TIGER RESERVE

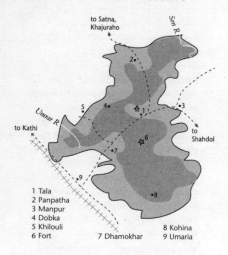

to Satna, Khajuraho
Son R.
to Kathi
Umrar R.
to Shahdol

1 Tala
2 Panpatha
3 Manpur
4 Dobka
5 Khilouli
6 Fort
7 Dhamokhar
8 Kohina
9 Umaria

Contact Field Director, Project Tiger,
Bandhavgarh Tiger Reserve, Tala,
P O Umaria, District Umaria 484661,
Madhya Pradesh Telefax (07627) 22214
Fax 22648
Area 1,161.47 sq km
Distance From Tala to: Umaria 34 km,
Katni 120 km, Jabalpur 180 km,
Khajuraho 300 km
Accommodation
Inside the reserve A forest rest-
house at Tala

Outside the reserve
Tala (STD code 07627)
Bandhavgarh Jungle Camp, Tel 65307
Fax 65365
Bandhavgarh Jungle Lodge, Tel 65317,
65320 [Delhi Tel (011) 6853760,
6858656 Fax 6865212]
Email T-Resorts@indiantiger.com
Bandhavgadh Safari Camp, Tel 65322
Kumkum Home, Tel 65324
Nature Heritage, Tel 65351
Patel Lodge, Tel 65323
Royal Retreat, Tel 65306
Royal Tiger Resort, Tel 65374-75
Tiger Den, Tel 65353
Tiger Trails (Indian Adventures),
Tel 65325-26 [Mumbai Tel (022)
6408742, 6433622, 6428244
Fax 6458401] Email iawr@vsnl.com
White Tiger Lodge, Tel 65308
[Bhopal headquarters Tel (0755)
778383; Mumbai Tel (022) 2187603
Fax 2160614]
Open season November to June
Best time to visit December to April
Climate November to February 5°C–25°C
March to June 16°C–42°C
Wildlife areas nearby
Panna Tiger Reserve
Contact Field Director, Project Tiger,
Panna Tiger Reserve, Panna Town,
District Panna 488001, Madhya Pradesh
Tel (07732) 52135
Distance Panna 18 km, Khajuraho 42 km
Best time to visit November to April
Mammals Tiger, Leopard, Wild Dog
(Dhole), Wolf, Sloth Bear, Sambar
Birds Bonelli's Eagle, Red Junglefowl,
Greater Racket-tailed Drongo
Ken Gharial Wildlife Sanctuary
Contact *See* Panna Tiger Reserve
Distance Panna Tiger Reserve 18 km
Best time to visit November to April
Reptiles Gharial, Mugger (Marsh
Crocodile)
Birds Sarus Crane, Demoiselle Crane,
Grey-headed Fish Eagle

PALAMAU TIGER RESERVE

1 Betla
2 Barwadih
3 Chhipadohar
4 Mundu
5 Garu
6 Maromar
7 Baresawar
8 Madgari
9 Neturhat

CONTACT Field Director, Project Tiger, Palamau Tiger Reserve, P O Daltonganj, District Palamau 822101, Jharkhand Tel (06562) 22650 Fax 22427

AREA 1,026.00 sq km

DISTANCE From Betla to: Daltonganj 25 km, Ranchi 150 km

ACCOMMODATION

Inside the reserve Forest rest-houses and lodges at Baresawar, Barwadih, Betla, Garu, Kerh, Maromar and other sites

Outside the reserve Several hotels at Daltonganj

OPEN SEASON October to May

BEST TIME TO VISIT December to April

CLIMATE October to November 14°C–32°C December to February 6°C–25°C March to May 18°C–42°C

WILDLIFE AREAS NEARBY

Hazaribagh Wildlife Sanctuary

Contact Divisional Forest Officer, Hazaribagh West Division, Hazaribagh 825301, Jharkhand Tel (06546) 23340

Distance Hazaribagh 22 km, Ranchi 110 km

Best time to visit November to April

Mammals Tiger, Leopard, Sambar

Reptiles Rock Python, Common Monitor

Birds Oriental Pied Hornbill, Changeable Hawk Eagle, Brown Fish Owl

KANHA TIGER RESERVE

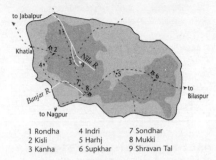

1 Rondha	4 Indri	7 Sondhar
2 Kisli	5 Harhj	8 Mukki
3 Kanha	6 Supkhar	9 Shravan Tal

CONTACT Field Director, Project Tiger, Kanha Tiger Reserve, P O Mandla, District Mandla 481661, Madhya Pradesh Tel (07642) 50760 Fax 51266

AREA 1,945 sq km

DISTANCE From Kisli to: Khatia 3 km, Mocha 8 km, Mandla 60 km, Jabalpur 160 km, Nagpur 260 km From Khatia to: Mukki 38 km

ACCOMMODATION

Inside the reserve Forest rest-houses and dormitories at Kisli, Mukki and Supkhar

Kisli (STD code 07649)
Baghira Loghuts (MP tourism), Tel 77227
Youth hostel (MP Tourism), Bhopal Tel (0755) 778383 [Mumbai Tel (022) 2187603 Fax 2160614]

Outside the reserve

Khatia (STD code 07649)
Chandan Motel, Tel 77220
Mogli Resort, Tel 77228

Mocha (STD code 07649)
Kipling Camp, Telefax 77219 [Kolkata Tel (033) 4734539 Fax 4731903]
Krishna Jungle Resort, Tel 77207-08
Tuli Tiger Resort, Tel 77221
Wild Chalet (Indian Adventures), Tel 77203, 77205 [Mumbai Tel (022) 6408742, 6433622, 6428244 Fax 6458401] Email iawr@vsnl.com

Mukki (STD code 07636)
Kanha Jungle Lodge, [Delhi Tel (011) 6853760, 6858656 Fax 6865212]
Royal Tiger Resort, Tel 56418, 56384

[Delhi Tel (011) 6149226/0116 Fax
6140903 Email tiger@nde.vsnl.net.in
OPEN SEASON October to June
BEST TIME TO VISIT December to March
CLIMATE October to November 14°C–30°C
December to February 3°C–25°C
March to June 18°C–42°C
WILDLIFE AREAS NEARBY
Pench Tiger Reserve *See p. 129*
Nagzira & Nawegaon *See below*

NAGZIRA WILDLIFE SANCTUARY & NAWEGAON NATIONAL PARK

CONTACT Deputy Conservator of Forests,
Wildlife Division, Ashirwad Bhavan,
Fulchur, Gondia, Maharashtra
Tel (07182) 26399
Email cfwl@nagpur.dot.net.in
OPEN SEASON October to June
BEST TIME TO VISIT December to April
CLIMATE October to November 14°C–30°C
December to February 5°C–27°C
March to April 18°C–42°C
Nagzira Wildlife Sanctuary
AREA 152.81 sq km
DISTANCE From main gate to:
Gondia 52 km, Nagpur 120 km
ACCOMMODATION
Inside the reserve A dormitory and
forest rest-houses (Nilay, Log Hut, Lata
Kunj, Madhu Kunj and Holiday Homes)
Outside the reserve
Gondia (STD code 07182)
Apsara, Tel 23790
Centaur, Tel 23740
Pacific, Tel 20006-07
Rasna, Tel 24395
Sagar, Tel 22383
Swaruchi, Tel 21131
Urvashi, Tel 22520, 23378
Nawegaon National Park
AREA 133.88 sq km
DISTANCE From main gate to:
Gondia 65 km, Nagpur 135 km
ACCOMMODATION
Inside the reserve Forest rest-houses
and youth hostel at Nawegaon; forest

bungalows near Nawegaon Lake
Outside the reserve *See* Nagzira
WILDLIFE AREAS NEARBY
Pench Tiger Reserve *See p. 129*
Tadoba-Andhari Tiger Reserve *See below*

TADOBA-ANDHARI TIGER RESERVE

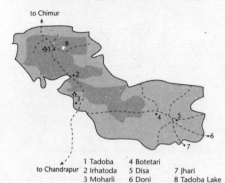

to Chimur

to Chandrapur

1 Tadoba	4 Botetari	
2 Irhatoda	5 Disa	7 Jhari
3 Moharli	6 Doni	8 Tadoba Lake

CONTACT Deputy Conservator of Forests,
Tadoba-Andhari Tiger Reserve, Opposite
Sancheti Chambers, Mul Road,
Chandrapur 442401, Maharashtra
Tel (07172) 51414
Email dcftatr@rediffmail.com
AREA 626.00 sq km
DISTANCE From Tadoba to: Moharli 20 km,
Chandrapur 45 km, Nagpur 200 km
ACCOMMODATION
Inside the reserve Forest rest-houses and
a youth hostel at Tadoba; forest rest-
house at Kolsa and Moharli; tent facilities
at Moharli on request
Outside the reserve
Chandrapur (STD code 07172)
Ganpati International, Tel 54454, 55264
Kundan Plaza, Tel 56606, 54822 Fax 54922
OPEN SEASON October to early June (closed
on Tuesdays and 31st December)
BEST TIME TO VISIT Late November to April
CLIMATE October to November 14°C–32°C
December to February 6°C–28°C
March to June 18°C–42°C
WILDLIFE AREAS NEARBY
Nagzira & Nawegaon *See above*

PENCH TIGER RESERVE

1 Halal   4 Karmajhiri   7 Payorthadi
2 Tikari   5 Chindia   8 Pulpuldoh
3 Rukhad   6 Turia   9 Totladoh

CONTACT Field Director, Project Tiger, Pench Tiger Reserve (MP), P O Barapathar, District Seoni 480661, Madhya Pradesh Tel (07692) 23794 Fax 21180 Email penchtr@bom6.vsnl.net.in

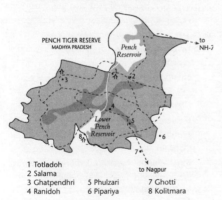

1 Totladoh
2 Salama
3 Ghatpendhri   5 Phulzari   7 Ghotti
4 Ranidoh   6 Pipariya   8 Kolitmara

CONTACT Field Director, Project Tiger, Pench Tiger Reserve (Mah), Zero Mile, Nagpur 440001, Maharashtra Tel (0712) 524727 Fax 552518 Email cfwl@nagpur.dot.net.in OR cf@wildlife-vidarbha.org

AREA 1,015.11 sq km

DISTANCE From Turia (MP) gate to: Khawasa 12 km, Nagpur 80 km, Jabalpur 190 km From Pipariya (Maharashtra) to: Totladoh 15 km, Ramtek 33 km, Nagpur 65 km From Totladoh (Maharashtra) to: Seoni 30 km, Nagpur 95 km, Jabalpur 200 km

ACCOMMODATION

Inside the reserve

Madhya Pradesh Forest rest-houses at Karmajhiri and Rukhad

Maharashtra Hornbill Nest forest rest-house at Kolitmara; forest rest-house and irrigation department rest-house at Totladoh, tents on request

Outside the reserve

Forest rest-houses at Chorbauli, Khawasa, Mogarkasa, Paoni and Sillari

Ramtek Holiday Resort (MTDC), Tel (07114) 55620, 55625 [Mumbai Tel (022) 2027762, 2027784]

OPEN SEASON Mid-October to June

BEST TIME TO VISIT December to March

CLIMATE October to November 15°C–30°C December to February 6°C–27°C March to June 20°C–42°C

WILDLIFE AREAS NEARBY

Nagzira & Nawegaon *See p. 128*
Kanha Tiger Reserve *See p. 127*

MELGHAT TIGER RESERVE

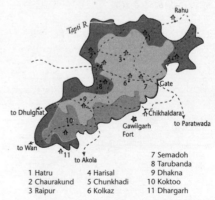

1 Hatru   4 Harisal   7 Semadoh
2 Chaurakund   5 Chunkhadi   8 Tarubanda
3 Raipur   6 Kolkaz   9 Dhakna
    10 Koktoo
    11 Dhargarh

CONTACT Field Director and Conservator of Forests, Project Tiger, Melghat Tiger Reserve, Amravati Camp, Amravati 444602, Maharashtra Tel (0721) 662792, 662680 Email meltiger@bom6.vsnl.net.in

AREA 1,676.93 sq km

DISTANCE From Semadoh tourist complex to:

Chikhaldara 25 km, Paratwada 50 km, Amravati 100 km, Badnera 110 km, Nagpur 230 km

ACCOMMODATION

Inside the reserve Forest rest-houses at Chaurakund, Chunkhadi, Dhakna, Dhargad, Hatru, Koktoo, Kolkaz, Makhla, Raipur and Tarubanda; dormitory at Semadoh; forest huts and tent accommodation at Harisal

Outside the reserve

Chikhaldara (STD code 07220)
Forest rest-house and PWD (Public Works Department) rest-house
Green Valleys Resort, Tel 20215, 20218
MTDC resort, Tel 20234, 20263 [MTDC Mumbai Tel (022) 2027762, 2027784]

OPEN SEASON October to June

BEST TIME TO VISIT December to April

CLIMATE October to November 16°C–34°C December to February 8°C–30°C March to June 18°C–42°C

EASTERN ZONE

NAMDAPHA TIGER RESERVE

Foreign nationals require Restricted Area Permits

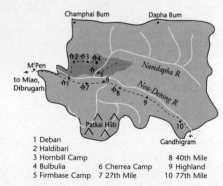

Champhai Bum   Dapha Bum

M'Pen
to Miao,
Dibrugarh

Namdapha R.

Noa-Dehing R.

Patkai Hills

Gandhigram

1 Deban
2 Haldibari
3 Hornbill Camp
4 Bulbulia   6 Cherrea Camp   8 40th Mile
5 Firmbase Camp   7 27th Mile   9 Highland
                                     10 77th Mile

CONTACT Field Director, Project Tiger, Namdapha Tiger Reserve, P O Miao, District Changlang 792122, Arunachal Pradesh Telefax (03807) 22249. Restricted Area Permits issued by the

Resident Commissioner, Arunachal Pradesh, Arunachal Bhavan, Kautilya Marg, New Delhi 110021 Tel (011) 3013915, 3012153

AREA 1,985.23 sq km

DISTANCE From Deban to: Miao 26 km, Margherita 70 km, Digboi 85 km, Tinsukia 135 km, Dibrugarh 175 km

ACCOMMODATION

Inside the reserve Forest rest-houses and dormitory at Deban; forest rest-houses at Bulbulia, 40th Mile Camp, Firmbase Camp, Haldibari, Hornbill Camp and 27th Mile Camp

Outside the reserve Forest rest-houses at Miao and Namchik; several lodges at Digboi, Margherita, Miao and Tinsukia

OPEN SEASON November to May

BEST TIME TO VISIT Mid-November to April

CLIMATE November to February 2°C–22°C March to May 10°C–28°C

WILDLIFE AREAS NEARBY

Dibru-Saikhowa National Park
Contact Divisional Forest Officer, Tinsukia Wildlife Division, P O Tinsukia 786125, Assam Tel (0374) 331472
Distance Tinsukia 12 km
Best time to visit November to March
Mammals Asian Water Buffalo, Gangetic Dolphin, Asian Elephant, Tiger, Hog-deer
Birds Bengal Florican, Swamp Francolin, Black-necked Stork, Marsh Babbler

Mehao Wildlife Sanctuary
Contact Assistant Conservator of Forests (SFS), P O Roing, District Dibang Valley, Arunachal Pradesh Tel (03803) 22408
Distance Roing 20 km, Tinsukia 120 km
Best time to visit November to March
Mammals Clouded Leopard, Hoolock Gibbon, Musk Deer, Spotted Linsang
Birds Great Peacock Pheasant

Dibang Wildlife Sanctuary
Contact Divisional Forest Officer (WL), Mehao WLS Division, P O Roing, District Dibang Valley, Arunachal Pradesh Tel (03803) 22408
Distance Anini 45 km, Tinsukia 225 km

Best time to visit November to March
Mammals Clouded Leopard, Hoolock
Gibbon, Binturong
Birds Wreathed Hornbill, Temminck's
Tragopan, Pied Falconet

KAZIRANGA NATIONAL PARK

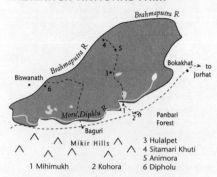

1 Mihimukh
2 Kohora
3 Hulalpet
4 Sitamari Khuti
5 Animora
6 Dipholu

CONTACT Director, Kaziranga National
Park, P O Bokakhat, District Golaghat
785612, Assam
AREA 471.71 sq km
DISTANCE From Mihimukh to: Kohora 2 km,
Bokakhat 25 km, Jorhat 98 km,
Guwahati 230 km
ACCOMMODATION
Outside the reserve
Kohora (STD code 0376)
A forest rest-house
Assam tourism hotels: Aranya Lodge,
Tel 2662429; Bonani, Bonashree and
Kunjaban, [Guwahati Tel (0361)
544475 Telefax 547102]
Wild Grass Resort, 5 km from Kohora,
Tel 2662011 [Guwahati Tel (0361)
546827 Fax 630465]
OPEN SEASON November to mid-April
BEST TIME TO VISIT December to March
CLIMATE November to February 6°C–30°C
March to April 14°C–34°C
WILDLIFE AREAS NEARBY
Panbari Forest
Distance Kohora 10 km
Best time to visit November to April
Mammals Hoolock Gibbon, Capped

Langur, Leopard-cat
Birds Grey Peacock Pheasant, Rufous-
bellied Eagle, Red-headed Trogon

KEIBUL-LAMJAO NATIONAL PARK

*Foreign nationals require permits for
visiting Manipur*
CONTACT Deputy Conservator of Forests,
Parks & Sanctuaries, Sanjenthong,
Imphal 795001, Manipur Tel (0385)
220854. For Manipur permits, contact
2 Sardar Patel Marg, Chanakyapuri,
New Delhi 110021 Tel (011) 3013009
AREA 40.00 sq km
DISTANCE From Sendra to: Imphal 32 km,
Kohima 160 km, Dimapur 225 km
ACCOMMODATION
Inside the reserve Forest rest-house
at Phubala; an observation tower
on Chingiao Hill
Outside the reserve Tourist bungalow on
Sendra Island, contact Hotel Imphal
Imphal (STD code 0385)
Anand Continental, Tel 223433
Excellency, Tel 223231
Hotel Imphal, Tel 220459, 223250
Fax 222629
Prince, Tel 220587
White Palace, Tel 220599
OPEN SEASON October to May
BEST TIME TO VISIT November to April
CLIMATE October to November 14°C–28°C
December to February 6°C–25°C
March to May 16°C–32°C

MANAS TIGER RESERVE

CONTACT Field Director, Project Tiger, Manas.
Tiger Reserve, P O Barpeta Road, District
Barpeta 781315, Assam
Tel (03666) 61413 Fax 32253
AREA 2,840.00 sq km
DISTANCE From Mothanguri to:
Bansbari gate 20 km, Barpeta Road
40 km, Guwahati 180 km
ACCOMMODATION
Inside the reserve Upper Bungalows
at Mothanguri

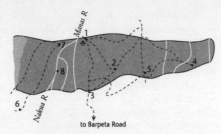

to Barpeta Road

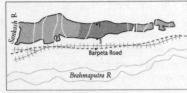

1 Mothanguri   4 Koklabari
2 Uchlia   5 Bhuyanpara   7 Gabaru Khunda
3 Bansbari   6 Panbari   8 Kapurpura

Outside the reserve

Bansbari Golden Langur Resort (Assam tourism), [Guwahati Tel (0361) 544475 Telefax 547102]

Barpeta Road Barpeta Tourist Lodge, [Guwahati Tel (0361) 546827 Fax 630465]

OPEN SEASON November to May

BEST TIME TO VISIT December to March

CLIMATE November to February 6°C–28°C March to May 15°C–34°C

WILDLIFE AREAS NEARBY

Dipar Beel Bird Sanctuary

Contact Divisional Forest Officer, Assam State Zoo Division, R G Baruah Road, Guwahati 781024, Assam Tel (0361) 261363

Distance Guwahati 12 km

Best time to visit November to March

Birds Greater Adjutant, Lesser Adjutant, Fulvous Whistling-duck, Pied Harrier, Pallas's Fish Eagle

Orang National Park

Contact Divisional Forest Officer, Mangaldoi Wildlife Division, P O Mangaldoi, Darrang 784125, Assam Tel (0914) 22065

Distance Tezpur 70 km, Guwahati 110 km

Best time to visit November to April

Mammals One-horned Rhinoceros, Asian Elephant, Tiger, Swamp Deer (Barasingha)

Birds White Pelican, Greater Adjutant, Lesser Adjutant, Black Stork

Laokhowa Wildlife Sanctuary

Contact Divisional Forest Officer, Nagaon Wildlife Division, P O & District Nagaon 782001, Assam Tel (03672) 23104

Distance Nagaon 40 km, Guwahati 170 km

Best time to visit November to mid-April

Mammals Asian Water Buffalo, One-horned Rhinoceros

Birds Black Stork, Greater Adjutant, Pied Harrier

Nameri National Park

Contact Divisional Forest Officer, Western Assam Wildlife Division, P O Koliabhomora, Tezpur 784001, Assam Tel (03712) 20854

Distance Tezpur 38 km

Best time to visit November to April

Mammals Tiger, Slow Loris

Birds Ibisbill, White-winged Duck, Rufous-necked Hornbill, Wreathed Hornbill, Collared Falconet

Pakhui Wildlife Sanctuary

Contact Divisional Forest Officer, Pakhui Wildlife Sanctuary Division, P O Seijusa, District West Kameng 790103, Arunachal Pradesh

Distance Tezpur 75 km, Itanagar 125 km

Best time to visit November to March

Mammals Tiger, Asian Elephant, Slow Loris, Leopard-cat

Birds Wreathed Hornbill, Rufous-necked Hornbill, Rufous-bellied Eagle

BUXA TIGER RESERVE & JALDAPARA WILDLIFE SANCTUARY

CONTACT

Buxa Field Director, Project Tiger, Buxa Tiger Reserve, P O Alipur Duar Court, District Jalpaiguri 736122, West Bengal

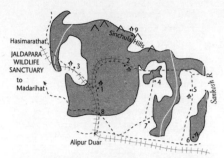

Hasimarathat
JALDAPARA
WILDLIFE
SANCTUARY
to
Madarihat

Sinchula Hills

Sankosh R.

Alipur Duar

1 Rajabhatkhawa	4 Kartika	7 Samuktlot
2 Jairo	5 Kumargram	8 Main gate
3 Kalchini	6 Sibunglow	9 Buxa Duar

Tel (03564) 56333 Fax 55577
Email buxatiger@dte.vsnl.net.in
Jaldapara Divisional Forest Officer,
Cooch-Behar Division, P O & District
Cooch-Behar, West Bengal
Telefax (03582) 27185
Email dfocob@dte.vsnl.net.in
OPEN SEASON October to May
BEST TIME TO VISIT December to April
CLIMATE October to November 15°C–30°C
December to February 6°C–27°C
March to May 15°C–34°C
Buxa Tiger Reserve
AREA 760.92 sq km
DISTANCE From main gate to: Alipur
Duar 25 km, Cooch-Behar 45 km,
Siliguri 165 km
ACCOMMODATION
Inside the reserve Forest rest-houses
and dormitories at Buxa Duar and
Rajabhatkhawa; forest rest-houses
at Jairo and Sibunglow
Outside the reserve Several hotels at
Alipur Duar and Cooch-Behar
Jaldapara Wildlife Sanctuary
AREA 216.51 sq km
DISTANCE From Hollong gate to: Madarihat
10 km, Alipur Duar 40 km, Jalpaiguri 100
km, Siliguri 130 km, Bagdogra 145 km
ACCOMMODATION
Inside the reserve Forest rest-houses at
Hollong; forest bungalow and lodge
at Borodabari

Outside the reserve
Madarihat WBTDC tourist lodge,
Tel (03563) 62230 [Kolkata Tel (033)
2485917, 2488271 Fax 2485168]
WILDLIFE AREAS NEARBY
Manas Tiger Reserve *See p. 131*

SUNDERBANS TIGER RESERVE
Foreign nationals require entry permits

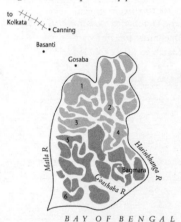

to
Kolkata
Canning
Basanti
Gosaba
Matla R.
Harinbhanga R.
Bagmara
Goashaba R.

BAY OF BENGAL

1 Sajnekhali	3 Netidhopani	5 Matla
2 Harinbhanga	4 Chandkhali	6 Mayadwip

CONTACT Field Director & Conservator of
Forests, Project Tiger, Sunderbans Tiger
Reserve, P O Canning Town, District 24
Parganas (South) 743329, West Bengal
Telefax (03218) 55280. For entry permits
contact Secretary, Department of Forest
and Tourism, Government of West
Bengal, Writers' Building, Kolkata 700001
Tel (033) 2215999
AREA 2,585.10 sq km
DISTANCE From Sajnekhali lodge to: Gosaba
45 km, Canning 100 km, Kolkata 160 km
ACCOMMODATION
Inside the reserve Private motorboats and
launches; entry permission required from
the Field Director (*See* Contact)
Sajnekhali (STD code 03463)
Pugmarks Resorts for stay on
boats, contact Kolkata Tel (033)

2873307 Telefax 2407737
Email pugmarks@vsnl.com
Tourist lodge (West Bengal tourism
department), Tel 52699 Fax 52398
[Kolkata Tel (033) 2488271, 2485917
Fax 2485168]

Outside the reserve
Several hotels at Canning

OPEN SEASON Mid-October to May

BEST TIME TO VISIT December to early April

CLIMATE October to November 18°C–32°C
    December to February 10°C–30°C
    March to May 18°C–35°C

SIMLIPAL TIGER RESERVE

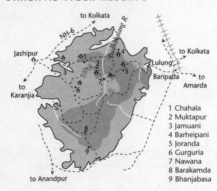

1 Chahala
2 Muktapur
3 Jamuani
4 Barheipani
5 Joranda
6 Gurguria
7 Nawana
8 Barakamda
9 Bhanjabasa

CONTACT Field Director, Project Tiger,
    Simlipal Tiger Reserve, P O Baripada,
    District Mayurbhanj 757002, Orissa
    Tel (06792) 52593 Fax 56705

AREA 2,750.00 sq km

DISTANCE From Nawana to: Baripada 45 km,
    Jashipur 50 km, Jamshedpur 175 km
    From Baripada to: Lulung 16 km,
    Jashipur 102 km, Kolkata 200 km

ACCOMMODATION

Inside the reserve Forest rest-houses,
    lodges and dormitories at Barheipani,
    Chahala, Gurguria, Joranda, Nawana and
    other sites. For reservation in Gurguria
    rest-house contact the Divisional Forest
    Officer, Karanjia Division, PO Karanjia,
    District Mayurbhanj, Orissa

Outside the reserve A forest rest-house

and private lodges in Jashipur
Polpola Retreat, *3 km west of Lulung*,
    (Pugmarks Resorts) Kolkata Tel (033)
    2873307 Telefax 2407737
    Email pugmarks@vsnl.com

Lulung Aranya Niwas (OTDC),
    [Bhubaneshwar Tel (0674)
    431299, 404715]

Baripada (STD code 06792)
Ambika Hotel, Tel 52557
Durga, Tel 53438

OPEN SEASON October to June

BEST TIME TO VISIT December to May

CLIMATE October to November 16°C–32°C
    December to February 12°C–30°C
    March to June 18°C–40°C

WILDLIFE AREAS NEARBY

Bhitarkanika & Gahirmatha
    See below

BHITARKANIKA WILDLIFE SANCTUARY & GAHIRMATHA MARINE WILDLIFE SANCTUARY

CONTACT Divisional Forest Officer, Mangrove
    Forest Division (Wildlife), Rajnagar,
    P O Rajnagar, District Kendrapara
    754225, Orissa Tel (06729) 72460

AREA (Bhitarkanika) 672.00 sq km;
    (Gahirmatha) 1,435.00 sq km

DISTANCE From Chandbali (1½ hrs by boat to
    the sanctuaries) to: Bhadrakh 45 km,
    Bhubaneshwar 140 km
    From Rajnagar (1½ hrs by boat to the
    sanctuaries) to: Gupti 25 km, Kendrapara
    40 km, Bhubaneshwar 130 km

ACCOMMODATION

Inside the reserve Forest rest-houses and
    inspection bungalows at Dangmal and
    Gupti in Bhitarkanika; Ekakula and
    Habalikhati in Gahirmatha. All these sites
    are accessible by boat from Chandbali
    and Rajnagar

Outside the reserve Forest rest-house
    at Chandbali; guest-houses and small
    lodges at Bhadrak, Rajnagar and
    Chandbali

OPEN SEASON October to May

BEST TIME TO VISIT December to March
CLIMATE October to November 18°C–32°C
December to February 14°C–30°C
March to May 20°C–38°C

NALABAN (CHILKA) WILDLIFE SANCTUARY

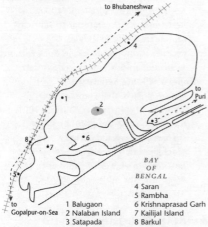

BAY
OF
BENGAL

1 Balugaon	4 Saran
2 Nalaban Island	5 Rambha
3 Satapada	6 Krishnaprasad Garh
	7 Kailijal Island
	8 Barkul

CONTACT Divisional Forest Officer, SFTRI Campus, Ghatikia, P O Barmunda Colony, Bhubaneshwar 751003, Orissa Tel (0674) 470149
  OR
Chilka Development Authority, BJ-45, BJB Nagar, Bhubaneshwar 751014, Orissa Tel (0674) 434044 Fax 434485 Email chilika@aiol.com
AREA 15.53 sq km
DISTANCE From Nalaban Island (by boat) to: Barkul 12 km, Balugaon 14 km, Satapada 18 km
From Satapada to: Barkul 28 km (by boat), Puri 48 km, Bhubaneshwar 100 km
From Balugaon to: Barkul 7 km, Rambha 28 km, Bhubaneshwar 95 km
From Rambha to: Gopalpur-on-Sea 50 km, Bhubaneshwar 130 km
ACCOMMODATION
  Outside the reserve OTDC tourist lodges:
    [OTDC Bhubaneshwar Tel (0674) 431299, Delhi Tel (011) 3364580]

Barkul Panthaniwas, Tel (06756) 20488
Rambha Panthaniwas, Tel (06810) 57346
Satapada Panthaniwas, Tel (0674) 432177
Balugaon Ashoka, Tel (06756) 20408-09
Puri (STD code 06752)
Derby, Tel 23961
Holiday Resort, Tel 22440 Fax 24370
Hotel Beach Hut, Tel 25704
Mayfair Beach Resort, Tel 24041 Fax 24242
Panthaniwas, Tel 22562
Seagull, Tel 23618
Toshali Sands, Tel 22888 Fax 23899
Z Hotel, Tel 22554
Gopalpur-on-Sea (STD code 0680)
Hotel Sagar, Tel 282327
Motel Mermaid, Tel 282050
Oberoi Palm Beach, Tel 282021
  Fax 282300 [Delhi Tel (011)
  4363030 Fax 4360484]
Song of the Sea, Tel 282347
OPEN SEASON October to June
BEST TIME TO VISIT December to March
CLIMATE October to November 20°C–32°C
December to February 14°C–30°C
March to June 20°C–37°C
WILDLIFE AREAS NEARBY
  Nandankanan Wildlife Sanctuary
    Contact Conservator of Forests (WL) and Ex-Officio Director, Nandankanan Zoological Park, Bhubaneshwar, at Mayurbhawan, P O Saheednagar, District Khurda 751007, Orissa
    Distance Bhubaneshwar 24 km, Balugaon 100 km
    Best time to visit Throughout the year
    Birds Red Junglefowl, Crested Serpent Eagle, Shikra, Greater Coucal
  Pulicat Lake Wildlife Sanctuary
    Contact Divisional Forest Officer (Wildlife Management), Sullurpet, District Nellore 524001, Andhra Pradesh Tel (08623) 62158
    Distance Chennai 45 km
    Best time to visit October to March
    Mammals Blackbuck, Jackal, Wild Boar
    Birds Greater Flamingo, Lesser Flamingo, Eurasian Curlew, Asian Dowitcher

SOUTHERN ZONE

NAGARJUNASAGAR-SRISAILAM TIGER RESERVE

1 Nagarjunasagar   5 Egalapenta
2 Sirigiripadu   6 Srisailam
3 Amrabad   7 Sundipenta
4 Mannanur   8 Chintala

CONTACT Field Director, Project Tiger, Nagarjunasagar-Srisailam Tiger Reserve, Srisailam Dam (East) 512102, Andhra Pradesh Tel (08524) 86089 Fax 86071

AREA 3,568.09 sq km

DISTANCE From Srisailam to: Markapur 85 km, Kurnool 190 km, Hyderabad 250 km

ACCOMMODATION

Inside the reserve Forest rest-houses, dormitories and APTDC properties at Nagarjunasagar and Srisailam. APTDC Hyderabad Tel (040) 3453036, 3450165 Telefax 3453086

Nagarjunasagar (STD code 08680) Punnami Hill Colony, Tel 76540 Punnami Hotel, Tel (08642) 42472 Vijay Vihar Complex, Tel 77361-62

Srisailam Ganga Sadan, Tel (08524) 87869, 87879

Outside the reserve

Forest rest-house at Mannanur

OPEN SEASON Throughout the year

BEST TIME TO VISIT December to April

CLIMATE March to June 18°C–42°C
July to October 18°C–38°C
November to February 15°C–32°C

WILDLIFE AREAS NEARBY

Rollapadu Wildlife Sanctuary
Contact Divisional Forest Officer (Wildlife Management), Atmakur, Kurnool 518422, Andhra Pradesh Tel (08516) 83337
Distance Nandikotkur 18 km, Atmakur 45 km, Srisailam 140 km
Best time to visit October to February
Mammals Wolf, Blackbuck
Reptiles Common Monitor, Rock Python
Birds Indian Bustard, Lesser Florican

Kolleru Wildlife Sanctuary
Contact Divisional Forest Officer (Wildlife Management), Eluru 534001, Andhra Pradesh Tel (08812) 32356
Distance Vijaywada 60 km, Machilipatnam 70 km
Best time to visit Mid-October to March
Birds Spot-billed Pelican, Painted Stork, Asian Openbill, Ruddy Shelduck

RANGANATHITTU WILDLIFE SANCTUARY

CONTACT Assistant Conservator of Forests, Wildlife Sub-division, Aranya Bhavan, Ashokpuram, Mysore 570008, Karnataka Tel (0821) 481159 Fax 489110

AREA 0.67 sq km

DISTANCE Srirangapatnam 3 km, Mysore 16 km, Bangalore 115 km

ACCOMMODATION

Inside the reserve One forest rest-house

Outside the reserve

Srirangapatnam (STD code 08236) Amblee Holiday Resort, Tel 52326 Hotel Mayura River View (KSTDC), Tel 52114

Mysore (STD code 0821) Hotel Mayura Hoysala (KSTDC), Tel 425349
King's Kourt, Tel 421142
Lalita Mahal Palace, Tel 571265 Fax 571770
Palace Plaza, Tel 430034
Quality Inn Southern Star, Tel 438141 Fax 421689
Rajendra Vilas Palace, Tel 520690

Ramanshree Comforts, Tel 522202
The Paradise, Tel 410366
OPEN SEASON Throughout the year
BEST TIME TO VISIT
May to September (nesting waterbirds),
December to February (wintering birds)
CLIMATE March to October 18°C–35°C
November to February 15°C–30°C
WILDLIFE AREAS NEARBY
Kokrebellur (waterbird nesting site)
Distance Bangalore 70 km
Best time to visit May to October
Mammals Jackal, Wild Boar
Birds Spot-billed Pelican, Painted
Stork, Black Ibis

NAGARHOLE NATIONAL PARK

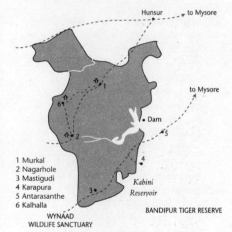

1 Murkal
2 Nagarhole
3 Mastigudi
4 Karapura
5 Antarasanthe
6 Kalhalla

CONTACT Deputy Conservator of Forests
(Wildlife Division), Hunsur 571105,
Mysore District, Karnataka
Tel (08222) 52041
AREA 643.39 sq km
DISTANCE From Nagarhole to: Kutta 10 km,
Karapur 25 km, Mysore 90 km,
Bangalore 220 km
ACCOMMODATION
Inside the reserve Forest rest-houses at
Kalhalla, Murkal and Nagarhole; bungalows
and dormitories at Nagarhole. Advisable
to arrive at Nagarhole gate well before

dusk as elephant blocks are common on
the park road leading to lodges; the road
closes at 6 pm
Outside the reserve
Karapur Kabini River Lodge (Jungle
Lodges), Tel (08228) 52160, 44405
[Bangalore Tel (080) 5597025
Fax 5586163]
Veeranahosahalli Jungle Inn,
Tel (08222) 46022, 52781
[Bangalore Tel (080) 2243172,
2238745 Fax 2235666]
Email jungle_inn@hotmail.com
OPEN SEASON Throughout the year
BEST TIME TO VISIT November to February,
May to August
CLIMATE March to June 18°C–35°C
July to October 16°C–34°C
November to February 14°C–30°C
WILDLIFE AREAS NEARBY
Wynaad Wildlife Sanctuary
Contact Wildlife Warden, Wynaad
Wildlife Division, P O Sultan's Battery,
Wynaad 673592, Kerala
Tel (0493) 620454
Distance Sultan's Battery 2 km,
Kozhikode (Calicut) 100 km
Best time to visit November to April
Mammals Asian Elephant, Gaur (Indian
Bison), Indian Giant Squirrel
Birds Malabar Pied Hornbill, Rufous-
bellied Eagle, Grey-headed Bulbul,
Spangled Drongo, Hill Myna
Bandipur Tiger Reserve *See below*
Mudumalai Wildlife Sanctuary *See p. 138*

BANDIPUR TIGER RESERVE
CONTACT Field Director, Project Tiger,
Bandipur Tiger Reserve, Aranya Bhavan,
Ashokapuram, Mysore 570008, Karnataka
Telefax (0821) 480901
Email fdptmys@blr.vsnl.net.in
OR
Deputy Conservator of Forests, Project
Tiger Division, Gundlupet 571111,
Mysore District, Karnataka
Tel (08229) 22260

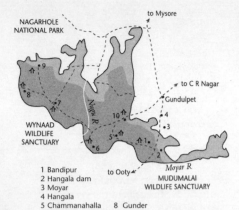

1 Bandipur
2 Hangala dam
3 Moyar
4 Hangala
5 Chammanahalla
6 Moolehole
7 Kalkere
8 Gunder
9 N Begur
10 Gopalaswamy Betta

MUDUMALAI
WILDLIFE SANCTUARY

AREA 874.00 sq km

DISTANCE From Bandipur tourist reception
centre to: Gundulpet 20 km, Mysore
78 km, Bangalore 210 km

ACCOMMODATION

Inside the reserve Forest rest-houses,
lodges, cottages and dormitories in
the Bandipur tourist complex area;
forest rest-houses at Chammanahalla,
Gopalaswamy Betta, Gunder,
Kakanhalla, Kalkere, Moolehole
and N Begur

Outside the reserve Between 4 km to
10 km from the Bandipur tourist complex
Bush Betta, [Bangalore Tel (080)
5512631 Fax 5593451]
Hotel Mayura Prakruti (KSTDC),
Tel (08229) 7301 [Bangalore Tel (080)
2212901, 2275869; Mysore Tel (0821)
442096 Fax 441833]
Tiger Ranch, [Bangalore Tel (080)
3374558 Fax 3373508]
Tusker Trails, [Bangalore Tel (080)
3342862]
See also Mudumalai below

OPEN SEASON Throughout the year

BEST TIME TO VISIT January to May,
September to October

CLIMATE March to October 18°C–35°C
November to February 12°C–30°C

WILDLIFE AREAS NEARBY
Wynaad Wildlife Sanctuary See p. 137

MUDUMALAI WILDLIFE SANCTUARY

CONTACT Wildlife Warden, Mahalingam
Building, P O Mount Stuart Hill, Coonor
Road, Udhagamandalam (Ooty) 643001,
Nilgiris District, Tamil Nadu
Tel (0423) 44098

OR

Theppakadu Reception Centre, Mysore-
Ooty Road Tel (0423) 56235

AREA 217.70 sq km

DISTANCE From Theppakadu to: Masinagudi
7 km, Bokkapuram 11 km, Gudalur
16 km, Udhagamandalam 64 km,
Mysore 90 km, Bangalore 220 km

ACCOMMODATION

Inside the reserve Forest rest-houses
and bungalows at Abhayaranyam,
Kargudi and Theppakadu; Log House,
Morgan dormitory and Sylvan Lodge
at Theppakadu

Outside the reserve
Masinagudi (STD code 0423)
Belleview, Tel 56351
Dreamland Hotel, Tel 56127
Hotel Tamil Nadu, Tel 56249
Mountania Resthouse, Tel 56337
Bokkapuram (STD code 0423)
Bamboo Banks, Tel 56222
Blue Valley Resorts, Tel 56244
Chital Walk, Tel 56256
Forest Hills Guesthouse, Tel 56216
Jungle Hut, Telefax 56240 [Bangalore
Tel (080) 5463848]
Jungle Retreat, Tel 56470 Fax 56469
Monarch, Tel 56326

OPEN SEASON Throughout the year

BEST TIME TO VISIT February to May,
September to October

CLIMATE March to October 18°C–35°C
November to February 12°C–28°C

WILDLIFE AREAS NEARBY
Mukurthi National Park
Contact See Mudumalai's
Udhagamandalam address

Distance Udhagamandalam 25 km
Best time to visit December to May
Mammals Nilgiri Langur, Nilgiri Tahr,
Asian Elephant, Indian Giant Squirrel
Birds Sri Lanka Frogmouth, Black Eagle,
Nilgiri Wood Pigeon, White-bellied
Treepie, Grey Junglefowl

SILENT VALLEY NATIONAL PARK
Entry permits required
CONTACT Assistant Wildlife Warden, Silent
Valley Range, P O Mukkali, District
Palakkad, Kerala Tel (0492) 453225
AREA 89.52 sq km
DISTANCE From Mukkali (18 km from the
park) to: Manakkad 20 km, Palakkad
85 km, Coimbatore 150 km
ACCOMMODATION
Outside the reserve A forest rest-house at
Mukkali and some lodges at Manakkad
Palakkad (STD code 0492)
Ambadi, Tel 531244
Fort Palace, Tel 534621
Indraprastha, Tel 534641
KPM International, Tel 534601
OPEN SEASON October to May
BEST TIME TO VISIT December to April
CLIMATE October to November 16°C–30°C
December to February 14°C–28°C
March to May 18°C–32°C
WILDLIFE AREAS NEARBY
Eravikulam National Park *See below*
Indira Gandhi (Annamalai) &
Parambikulam *See below*

INDIRA GANDHI (ANNAMALAI) NATIONAL PARK & PARAMBIKULAM WILDLIFE SANCTUARY
CONTACT
Annamalai Wildlife Warden, 176
Meenkarai Road, Pollachi, District
Coimbatore 642001, Tamil Nadu
Tel (04259) 25356
Parambikulam Wildlife Warden/DFO,
Parambikulam Division,
P O Thunakkadavu, (Via) Pollachi,
District Pollachi 678661, Kerala

Tel (0425) 367233
AREA Annamalai 117.10 sq km
Parambikulam 285.00 sq km
DISTANCE
Annamalai From Topslip to:
Pollachi 36 km, Coimbatore 80 km,
Udhagamandalam 165 km
Parambikulam From Thunakkadavu to:
Topslip 12 km, Pollachi 48 km
ACCOMMODATION
Inside the reserve Forest rest-houses, log
huts and dormitories at Topslip, Ambuli
Illam and Anaipadi in Annamalai;
Thunakkadavu and Parambikulam in
Parambikulam Wildlife Sanctuary
Outside the reserve
Pollachi (STD code 04259)
Ashok, Tel 224483
KDK, Tel 226871
Krishna, Tel 225895
Manis, Tel 223041
New Abirami, Tel 229815
Sakthi, Tel 223050, 223060 Fax 224557
OPEN SEASON Throughout the year
BEST TIME TO VISIT December to April
CLIMATE March to October 14°C–32°C
November to February 6°C–24°C
WILDLIFE AREAS NEARBY
Eravikulam National Park *See below*

ERAVIKULAM NATIONAL PARK
CONTACT Assistant Wildlife Warden,
Eravikulam National Park, P O Vagavurai,
Munnar, District Idukki 685612, Kerala
Tel (04865) 30487
AREA 97.00 sq km
DISTANCE From the main entrance to:
Munnar 15 km, Cochin 150 km
ACCOMMODATION
Inside the reserve
A forest rest-house at Rajamalai
Outside the reserve
Munnar (STD code 04865)
Copper Castle, Tel 530633
Edassery Eastend, Tel 530451
Hill View, Tel 530567
Poopada Tourist Home, Tel 530223

Residency, Tel 530317
Royal Retreat, Tel 530240
OPEN SEASON Throughout the year
BEST TIME TO VISIT November to April
CLIMATE March to October 12°C–28°C
November to February 5°C–22°C
WILDLIFE AREAS NEARBY
Chinar Wildlife Sanctuáry
Contact Wildlife Warden, Eravikulam
Wildlife Division, P O Munnar, District
Idukki 685603, Kerala Tel (04865) 30487
Distance Udumalpet 30 km,
Munnar 55 km, Pollachi 55 km
Best time to visit November to April
Mammals Asian Elephant, Leopard,
Grizzled Giant Squirrel
Birds Chestnut-headed Bee-eater,
Malabar Pied Hornbill, Grey Junglefowl
Thattekadu Wildlife Sanctuary
Contact Wildlife Warden, Idukki Wildlife
Division, P O Painavu, District Idukki
685603, Kerala Tel (04862) 32271
Distance Kothamangalam 16 km,
Munnar 65 km, Cochin 80 km
Best time to visit November to April
Mammals Lion-tailed Macaque,
Indian Giant Squirrel, Small
Travancore Flying Squirrel
Birds Malabar Trogon, Sri Lanka
Frogmouth, Malabar Grey Hornbill,
Black Baza

PERIYAR TIGER RESERVE
CONTACT Field Director, Project Tiger, Periyar
Tiger Reserve, Aranya Bhavan, Forest
Complex, S H Mount, P O Kottayam
686006, Kerala Tel (0481) 562940
Fax 569217
OR
Wildlife Preservation Officer, Periyar Tiger
Reserve, P O Kumily, Thekkady, District
Idukki 685536, Kerala
Tel (0486) 322027
AREA 777 sq km
DISTANCE From Thekkady tourist centre to:
Kumily 3 km, Kottayam 112 km, Madurai
140 km, Cochin 185 km

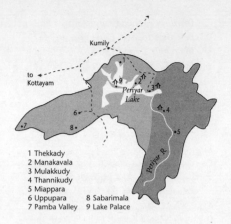

1 Thekkady
2 Manakavala
3 Mulakkudy
4 Thannikudy
5 Miappara
6 Uppupara   8 Sabarimala
7 Pamba Valley 9 Lake Palace

ACCOMMODATION
Inside the reserve Forest rest-houses and
dormitories at Manakavala, Mulakkudy
and Thannikudy
Thekkady (STD code 0486)
KTDC hotels, Tel 322026 Fax 322282
Email ktdc@giasmel01.vsnl.net.in
Aranya Nivas, Tel 322023 Fax 322282
Lake Palace, Tel 322024 Fax 322282
Periyar House, Tel 322026 Fax 322526
Outside the reserve
Several resorts between Kumily and
Thekkady park entrance (STD code 0486)
Hotel Ambadi, Tel 322193-94
Shalimar Spice Garden, Tel 322132
Spice Village, Tel 322314-15 Fax 322317
[Central reservation office at Kochi, Tel
(0484) 668221, 668421 Fax 668001]
Taj Garden Retreat, Tel 322401,
322273 Fax 322106
Email retreat.thekkady@tajhotels.com
Kumily (STD code 0486)
Cardamom County, Tel 322816
Fax 322807
Green Garden Cottage, Tel 322749
Lake Queen Tourist Home, Tel 322084
Regent Tower, Tel 322570
Rolex Tourist Home, Tel 322081
OPEN SEASON Throughout the year
BEST TIME TO VISIT December to April
CLIMATE March to October 18°C–34°C
November to February 10°C–28°C

POINT CALIMERE WILDLIFE SANCTUARY & VEDANTHANGAL WILDLIFE SANCTUARY

OPEN SEASON Throughout the year

BEST TIME TO VISIT

Point Calimere November to April

Vedanthangal October to February

CLIMATE March to October 20°C–40°C
November to February 15°C–32°C

Point Calimere Wildlife Sanctuary

CONTACT Wildlife Warden, Point Calimere
WLS, Collectorate Complex,
Nagapattinam 611001, District
Nagapattinam, Tamil Nadu
Tel (04365) 22349

AREA 17.26 sq km

DISTANCE From Flamingo House to:
Vedaranyam 11 km, Nagapattinam 50 km,
Thanjavur 90 km, Chennai 360 km

ACCOMMODATION

Inside the reserve Flamingo House
(locally Poonarai Illam), a forest rest-
house at Kodikkarai

Outside the reserve
Several lodges and hotels at
Vedaranyam and Nagapattinam
Thanjavur (STD code 04362)
Hotel Tamil Nadu, Tel 31421
Pandiyan Residency, Tel 31295
Purushutam, Tel 31844

Vedanthangal Wildlife Sanctuary

CONTACT Wildlife Warden, 259 Anna
Salai, 4th floor, D M S Compound,
Teynampet, Chennai

Tel (044) 4321471

AREA 0.30 sq km

DISTANCE Chingleput 34 km,
Mamallapuram 45 km, Chennai 82 km

ACCOMMODATION

Outside the reserve
A forest rest-house 1 km from
Vedanthangal tank
Mamallapuram (STD code 04114)
Ideal Beach Resort, Tel 42240
Fax 42243
Mamalla Bhavan, Tel 42260
Sea Breeze, Tel 43035 Fax 43065
Surya, Tel 42292
Temple Bay Ashok Beach Resort,
Tel 42251, 42257

WILDLIFE AREAS NEARBY

Pulicat Lake Wildlife Sanctuary

See p. 135

Nellapatu Wildlife Sanctuary

Contact Divisional Forest Officer
(Wildlife Management), Sullurpet, District
Nellore 524001, Andhra Pradesh
Tel (08623) 62158

Distance Sullurpet 15 km, Nellore 78 km,
Chennai 105 km

Best time to visit November to March

Mammals Jackal, Jungle Cat, Wild Boar,
Smooth Indian Otter

Birds Spot-billed Pelican, Painted
Stork, Great Cormorant, Indian
Cormorant, Darter, Eurasian Spoonbill,
Asian Openbill, Black-headed Ibis,
Grey Heron, Purple Heron, Great Egret

INTERNET DISCUSSION GROUPS

The following are interactive internet discussion groups on Indian wildlife and environment.
To subscribe to any of these (membership is free), send an email to the address given alongside
each group; do put in your name and, if possible, place of residence.

Birdsofbombay birdsofbombay-subscribe@yahoogroups.com
delhibird delhibird-subscribe@yahoogroups.com
Mumbainaturalists mumbainaturalists-subscribe@yahoogroups.com
nathistory-india nathistory-india@princeton.edu
OrientalBirding orientalbirding-subscribe@yahoogroups.com

WILDLIFE & CONSERVATION ORGANIZATIONS

The following are some of India's organizations concerned with wildlife and conservation issues that can help provide information on Indian natural history and environment. Some of these* offer membership and/or subscription to their publication(s).

AARANYAK Samanwoy Path (Survey), Beltola, Guwahati 781028, Assam Tel (0361) 266087

ALIPURDUAR NATURE CLUB Newtown, P O Alipur Duar Court, District Jalpaiguri 736122, West Bengal Tel (03564) 56440 Fax 55364

BASTAR SOCIETY FOR CONSERVATION OF NATURE 'Jeevan Sadan', Nayapara, Jagdalpur 494001, Chattisgarh

BIRDWATCHER'S SOCIETY OF ANDHRA PRADESH (BSAP)* P O Box 45, Banjara Hills, Hyderabad 500034

OR

Aasheesh Pittie, 8-2-545 Prem Parvat, Road 7, Banjara Hills, Hyderabad 500034 Tel (040) 3352269 Fax 3356065 Email aasheesh@vsnl.in

BOMBAY ENVIRONMENT ACTION GROUP (BEAG) Room 54, 2nd Floor, Kalbadevi Municipal School, Mumbai 400002, Maharashtra Tel (022) 2423126 Fax 2426385 Email debi@beag.net

BOMBAY NATURAL HISTORY SOCIETY (BNHS)* Hornbill House, Dr Salim Ali Chowk, Opposite Lion Gate, S B Singh Road, Mumbai 400023 Tel (022) 2821811 Fax 2837615 Email bnhs@bom4.vsnl.net.in

CENTRE FOR ENVIRONMENT EDUCATION (CEE) Thaltej Tekra, Ahmedabad 380054, Gujarat Tel (079) 6858002-09 Fax 6858010 Email ceeindia@vsnl.com

CENTRE FOR HIMALAYAN ENVIRONMENT AND DEVELOPMENT Near Akashwani Kendra, Haldapani, Gopeshwar, District Chamoli 246401, Uttar Pradesh Tel (01372) 2366

CENTRE FOR SCIENCE & ENVIRONMENT (CSE)* 41, Tughlaqabad Institutional Area, New Delhi 110062 Tel (011) 6081110, 6081124 Fax 6085879 Email cse@cseindia.org

DELHIBIRD (northern India bird network), Flat 103, Block C-1, Mayfair Towers, Eros Garden, Charmwood Village, Surajkund Road, Faridabad 121005, Haryana Tel (0129) 5253294 Email nik@sapta.com

GUJARAT ECOLOGICAL EDUCATION & RESEARCH FOUNDATION Geer Foundation, Indroda Nature Park, Sector 9, Gandhinagar 382009, Gujarat Tel (02712) 21385 Fax 41128 Email geer@guj.nic.in

HIMALAYAN NATURE & ENVIRONMENT PRESERVATION SOCIETY Om Bhavan, Chaura Maidan, Shimla 171004, Himachal Pradesh Fax (0177) 211485

INDIAN NATIONAL TRUST FOR ART AND CULTURAL HERITAGE, THE (INTACH) "Sanskriti", P O Hazaribagh 825301, Bihar Fax (06546) 24228 Email Bulu@koel.indiax.com

INSTITUTE OF BIRD STUDIES & NATURAL HISTORY (KFI RISHI VALLEY TRUST) P O Rishi Valley, Chittoor District 517352, Andhra Pradesh Tel (08571) 26037 Fax 68622

KALPAVRIKSH* New Delhi B-25 Defence Colony, New Delhi 110024 Tel (011) 4624197 Email harmony@del2.vsnl.net.in Pune Apartment 5, Shree Dutta Krupa, 908 Deccan Gymkhana, Pune 411004 Telefax (020) 5654239 Email kvriksh@vsnl.com

M S SWAMINATHAN RESEARCH FOUNDATION 3rd Cross Street, Taramani Institutional Area, Chennai 600113, Tamil Nadu Tel (044) 2351698

MADRAS CROCODILE BANK Post Box No 4, Mamallapuram 603104, Tamil Nadu Tel (044) 4910910

MADRAS NATURALIST'S SOCIETY 8 Janaki Avenue, Abhirampuram, Chennai 600018, Tamil Nadu Tel (044) 4997614

NATIONAL SOCIETY OF THE FRIENDS OF THE TREES 3rd Floor, Union Co-operative Insurance Building, 23 P M Road, Fort, Mumbai 400001 Telefax (022) 2870860

NATURE & WILDLIFE CONSERVATION SOCIETY OF ORISSA Mayur Bhavan, Janpath, Shaheed Nagar, Bhubaneshwar 751007, Orissa Tel (0674) 53840

NATURE CONSERVATION SOCIETY I T O Road, Redma, Daltonganj 822101, Jharkhand Telefax (06562) 22722

NATURE CONSERVATION SOCIETY "Pratishtha", Bharat Nagar, Akoli Road, Near Sai Nagar, Amravati 444605 Maharashtra Email kishorrithe@yahoo.com

NATURE CONSERVATION SOCIETY OF NASIK Hemant Vihar, Plot No 13, Savarkar Nagar, Off Gangapur Road, Nasik 422005, Maharashtra Email wolfajay@hotmail.com

NATURE LOVERS CLUB – BELGAUM Environment Protection Cell, Biology Department, G S Science College Tilakwadi, Belgaum 590006, Karnataka

NATURES' BECKON Ward No 1, Datta Bari, P O Dhubri, Assam 783301 Tel (03662) 31067, 30076

*NEWSLETTER FOR BIRDWATCHERS** Navbharat Enterprises, 10 Sirur Park 'B' Street, Seshadripuram, Bangalore 560020 Tel (080) 3364142 Fax 3364697

NILGIRI WILDLIFE ASSOCIATION AND ENVIRONMENT ASSOCIATION c/o District Forest Office, Nilgiris North Division, Mount Stuart Hill, Udhagamandalam (Ooty) 643001, Tamil Nadu

RANTHAMBORE FOUNDATION
New Delhi 19 Kautilya Marg, Chanakyapuri, New Delhi 110021 Tel (011) 3016261 Fax 3019457
Sawai Madhopur 10 Bal Mandir Colony, Mantown, Sawai Madhopur 322001, Rajasthan Tel (07462) 20286

RHINO FOUNDATION, THE c/o The Assam Co Ltd, G Bordoloi Path, Bamunimaidam, Guwahati 781021 Tel (0361) 550257, 663339 Fax 550902

Email badru1@sancharnet.in

RISHI VALLEY EDUCATION CENTRE P O Rishi Valley, Chitoor District 517352, Andhra Pradesh Tel (08571) 22037 Fax 22818

SALIM ALI CENTRE FOR ORNITHOLOGY & NATURAL HISTORY (SACON) P O Kalampalayam, Coimbatore 641010, Tamil Nadu Tel (0422) 657102-06 Fax 657088 Email sacon@md3.vsnl.net.in

*SANCTUARY ASIA** 602 Maker Chambers V, Nariman Point, Mumbai 400021 Tel (022) 2830061/81 Fax 2874380 Email sanctuary@vsnl.com OR bittu@sanctuaryasia.com

TOURISM & WILDLIFE SOCIETY OF INDIA (TWSI) C-158 A, Dayanand Marg, Tilak Nagar, Jaipur 302004, Rajasthan Tel (0141) 621472

TRADE RECORDS ANALYSIS OF FLORA AND FAUNA IN COMMERCE (TRAFFIC), INDIA c/o WWF India, 172-B, Lodi Estate, New Delhi 110003 Tel (011) 4698578

VIDARBHA NATURE CONSERVATION SOCIETY Tidke Ashram, Near Ganeshpeth Police Station, Nagpur 440018, Maharashtra Tel (0712) 727363

WILD ORISSA Plot 3A, Janpath, Satya Nagar, Bhubaneshwar, Orrisa Tel (0674) 512044 Email surjitbhujabal@hotmail.com

WILDLIFE INSTITUTE OF INDIA (WII) P O Box 18, Chandrabani, Dehradun 248001, Uttaranchal Tel (0135) 640112-15 Fax 640117

WILDLIFE PROTECTION SOCIETY OF INDIA (WPSI) Thapar House, 124 Janpath, New Delhi 110001 Tel (011) 6213864 Fax 6464918

WILDLIFE TRUST OF INDIA P O 3150, New Delhi 110003 Tel (011) 6326025-26 Telefax 6326027

WORLD PHEASANT ASSOCIATION S-56/1, DLF III, Gurgaon 122002, Haryana Telefax (0124) 6562406 Email r_kaulhotmail.com

WORLD WIDE FUND FOR NATURE (WWF), INDIA
New Delhi 172-B, Lodi Estate, New Delhi 110003 Tel (011) 4633473, 4637586 Fax 4626837

Email wwfindia@vsnl.net
Maharashtra state office
WWF India, National Insurance Building,
2nd Floor, 204 Dr D N Road, Fort,
Mumbai 400001 Tel (022) 2078105,
2075142 Fax 2076037
Email wwfbombay@vsnl.com
*WWF India has branches in Bangalore,
Chennai, Guwahati, Hyderabad, Kolkata,*

Pune, Vadodara and several other towns
ZOOLOGICAL SURVEY OF INDIA **(ZSI)**
Prani Vigyan Bhavan, M Block, New
Alipore, Kolkata 700053, West Bengal
Tel (033) 4006893, 4008595
For publications contact
ZSI Publications Department, 13th Floor
M S O Building, 234/4 Acharya J C Bose
Marg, Kolkata 700020

SELECT BIBLIOGRAPHY

ALI, SALIM. *The Book of Indian Birds*. 12th edition.
Bombay: Bombay Natural History Society
(BNHS)/Oxford University Press (OUP), 1996

BAKER, E C STUART. *Fauna of British India:
Birds*. 8 vols. London: Taylor & Francis,
1922-1930

BEDI, RAJESH & RAMESH BEDI. *Indian Wildlife*.
New Delhi: Brijbasi Printers, 1984

BRANDER, A DUNBAR. *Wild Animals of Central
India*. London, 1923

BURTON, R G. *Sport and Wildlife in the Deccan*.
London: Hutchinson, 1928

CORBETT, JIM. *Jungle Lore*. Bombay: Oxford
University Press, 1953

DANIEL, J C, ed. *A Century of Natural History*.
Bombay: BNHS, 1983

GEE, E P. *The Wildlife of India*. New Delhi:
HarperCollins, 2000

GRIMMETT, R, CAROL INSKIPP AND TIM INSKIPP.
Birds of the Indian Subcontinent. New
Delhi: Oxford University Press, 1999

HAWKINS, R E. *Jim Corbett's India*. Bombay:
Oxford University Press, 1978

ISRAEL, S & TOBY SINCLAIR. *Indian Wildlife*.
Singapore: APA Productions, 1993

KAZMIERCZAK, KRYS & RAJ SINGH. *A Birdwatcher's
Guide to India*. New Delhi: Oxford
University Press, 2001

KEHIMKAR, ISAAC. *Common Indian Wild Flowers*.
Bombay: BNHS/Oxford University
Press, 2000

KOTHARI, A & B F CHHAPGAR, eds. *Salim Ali's
India*. Bombay: BNHS/Oxford University
Press, 1996

KOTHARI, ASHISH & ROSHNI KUTTY. *Protected
Areas in India: A Profile*. Pune:
Kalpavriksh, 2001

KRISHNAN, M. *Nights and Days: My Book on
India's Wildlife*. New Delhi: Vikas
Publishing House Pvt Ltd, 1989

MANFREDI, PAOLA, ed. *In Danger*. New Delhi:
Local Colour Private Limited in
association with Ranthambore
Foundation, 1997

PRATER S H. *The Book of Indian Animals*.
3rd edition. Bombay: BNHS/Oxford
University Press, 1971

RANJITSINH, M K. *The Indian Blackbuck*.
Dehradun: Nataraj Publishers, 1989

RATHORE, FATEH SINGH, TEJBIR SINGH & VALMIK
THAPAR. *With Tigers in the Wild*.
New Delhi: Vikas Publishing House
Pvt Ltd, 1983

SAHANI, K C. *The Book of Indian Trees*.
Bombay: BNHS/Oxford University
Press, 1998

SANKHALA, K. *Tiger!* Collins, 1978

SINGH, ARJAN. *Tiger Haven*. London:
MacMillan, 1973

SANDERSON, G P. *Thirteen Years Among the
Wild Beasts of India*. London, 1896

SESHADRI, B. *India's Wildlife and Wildlife
Reserves*. New Delhi: Sterling, 1986

THAPAR, VALMIK. *Tigers: The Secret Life*. New
Delhi: Oxford University Press, 1989

WHISTLER, HUGH. *The Popular Handbook of
Indian Birds*. London: Gurney and
Jackson, 1941

ACKNOWLEDGEMENTS

There are many I am grateful to for helping with this book.

First and foremost, I thank Deutsche Bank for supporting this project. Pavan Sukhdev's passion for the environment and his concern for wildlife conservation made this happen. Rajiv Baruah helped co-ordinate the project. The dovetailing of corporate thinking and environmental concerns is an encouraging prospect for India's wilderness.

The Forest & Wildlife Departments of all states, including the staff of Project Tiger Reserves and other Protected Areas helped with information. The *Project Tiger Status Report* (2001) of the Ministry of Environment and Forests, Government of India, was an invaluable source of reference. I am particularly grateful to Suresh Gairola, Nitin Kakodkar and A R Bharati in Maharashtra for their many suggestions.

I sincerely thank the Bombay Natural History Society (BNHS) for the numerous opportunities it offers for meaningful interaction. I especially thank J C Daniel, Dr Asad Rahmani, Dr S Balachandran, P B Shekhar, Naresh Chaturvedi, Isaac Kehimkar, Ranjit Manakadan, Supriya Jhunjhunwala, Dr Gayatri Ugra, Deepak Apte and Abhijit Malekar for their assistance.

Dr Ravi Chellam, Dr G S Rawat, Dr S A Hussain, Dr Kartik Shanker and Bivash Pandav from Wildlife Institute of India (WII), Dehradun, offered many worthy suggestions. The WII's *Envis Bulletin* (June, 2000) proved to be a precious reference source. Dr Anwaruddin Choudhury from the Rhino Foundation, Guwahati, and Dr Goutam Narayan readily helped with their intimate knowledge of India's enchanting north-east. My photographer-colleagues provided not just images but also chipped in with constructive inputs about the many reserves. Vivek Tiwari kindly let me use the nathistory-india internet group for information from members, while Bittu Sahgal and *Sanctuary* magazine were a great help. Manisha Shah helped with the maps and data gathering and I thank her for her hard work.

Ashish Kothari and Roshni Kutty from Kalpavriksh, Surjit Bhujabal and Mr Sethi from Wild Orissa, Shoaib Kader and Eric D'Cunha from Indian Adventures, Smaran Ghosal of Pugmarks Nature Resorts, Kolkata, were all a wealth of facts and figures and guided me to additional sources of information. Sterling Travels, Mumbai helped organize my trips. Other colleagues who assisted in myriad ways include Ravi Singh at Deutsche Bank, Mumbai, Debi Goenka, Gopal Bodhe, Dr B Dasgupta, Vivek Kulkarni, Vijay Awsare, Sunetro Ghosal, Dr Salil Choksi, Sanal Nair and Celine Anthony in Mumbai, Bholu Khan at Bharatpur, M S K Pasha in Delhi, Krupakar-Senani in Mysore, Vivek Sinha in Bangalore, Suresh Elamon in Thiruvananthapuram, A R Kshatriya at Dhrangadhara and Abdul Rauf Zargar in Leh.

Once again, it was a pleasure for me to work with IBH. Padmini Mirchandani's interest in the promotion of high-quality publications on Indian natural history augurs well for the environment. Meera Ahuja's enthusiasm and hawk-eye for detail, the co-operation of the two computer-savvy Sachins, and above all, my editors Lavanya Ray and Shikha Gupta, made a chaotic mass of data appear comprehensible.

My family's continuous support and patience, especially of my parents and my wife, have been inspirational and allowed me the liberty of continuing my romance with India's wilds. Above all, I dedicate this work to my little daughter, Yuhina, so animated and cheery, smiling amid her trials of life. I have an intense hope that she and her generation, India's children of today and tomorrow, shall learn to value, enjoy and help defend their priceless natural heritage.

SUNJOY MONGA

CREDITS *Photographs from PORPOISE PhotoStock except those marked with an asterisk*

INDEX *Page numbers in bold refer to illustrations*

For my little Yuhina

ISBN 81-7508-325-5

TEXT
© 2002 Sunjoy Monga

PUBLISHED BY
India Book House Pvt Ltd
412 Tulsiani Chambers
Nariman Point, Mumbai 400 021, India
Tel 91 22 284 0165   Fax 91 22 283 5099
E-mail ibhpub@vsnl.com